W9-CDM-775

Love Canal

WE'VE GOT BETTER
THINGS TO DO THAN
SIT AROUND AND BE
CONTAMINATED !!

GREAT DISASTERS
REFORMS and RAMIFICATIONS

Love Canal

Jennifer Bond Reed

CHELSEA HOUSE PUBLISHERS
Philadelphia

Frontispiece: Mark Zanatian waves a banner during a 1978 Love Canal protest. Zanatian is one of the children endangered by the chemicals in the Love Canal under 99th Street School.

CHELSEA HOUSE PUBLISHERS

Editor in Chief Sally Cheney
Director of Production Kim Shinners
Creative Manager Takeshi Takahashi
Manufacturing Manager Diann Grasse

Staff for LOVE CANAL

Assistant Editor Susan Naab
Picture Researcher Jaimie Winkler
Production Assistant Jaimie Winkler
Cover and Series Designer Takeshi Takahashi
Layout 21st Century Publishing and Communications, Inc.

Printed and bound in the United States of America.

First Printing

1 3 5 7 9 8 6 4 2

The Chelsea House World Wide Web address is
http://www.chelseahouse.com

Library of Congress Cataloging-in-Publication Data

Reed, Jennifer.
Love Canal / by Jennifer Reed.
v. cm. — (Great disasters, reforms and ramifications)
Includes bibliographical references and index.
Contents: 1. A mother's crusade — 2. Before the Love Canal crises — 3.Breaking news — 4. Children at risk — 5. The great escape — 6. The great debate — 7. Now what?
ISBN 0-7910-6742-4
1. Love Canal Chemical Waste Landfill (Niagara Falls, N.Y.) —Juvenile literature. 2. Chemical plants—Waste disposal—Health aspects—New York (State)—Niagara Falls—Juvenile literature. 3. Gibbs, Lois Marie—Juvenile literature. [1. Love Canal Chemical Waste Landfill (Niagara Falls, N.Y.) 2. Hazardous waste sites.] I. Title. II. Series.
TD181.N72 N513 2002
363.738'4'0974798—dc21

2001008373

Contents

GREAT DISASTERS
REFORMS and RAMIFICATIONS

THE *APOLLO I* AND
CHALLENGER DISASTERS

BHOPAL

THE BLACK DEATH

THE BLIZZARD OF 1888

THE BOMBING OF HIROSHIMA

THE CHERNOBYL NUCLEAR DISASTER

THE DUST BOWL

THE EXPLOSION OF TWA FLIGHT 800

THE *EXXON VALDEZ*

THE GALVESTON HURRICANE

THE GREAT CHICAGO FIRE

THE GREAT PLAGUE AND
FIRE OF LONDON

THE *HINDENBURG*

THE HOLOCAUST

THE INFLUENZA PANDEMIC OF 1918

THE IRISH POTATO FAMINE

THE JOHNSTOWN FLOOD

LOVE CANAL

THE MUNICH OLYMPICS

NUCLEAR SUBMARINE DISASTERS

THE OKLAHOMA CITY BOMBING

PEARL HARBOR

THE SALEM WITCH TRIALS

THE SAN FRANCISCO EARTHQUAKE
OF 1906

THE SPANISH INQUISITION

THE STOCK MARKET CRASH OF 1929

TERRORISM

THREE MILE ISLAND

THE *TITANIC*

THE TRIANGLE SHIRTWAIST COMPANY
FIRE OF 1911

THE WACO SIEGE

THE WORLD TRADE CENTER BOMBING

Jill McCaffrey
National Chairman
Armed Forces Emergency Services
American Red Cross

Introduction

Disasters have always been a source of fascination and awe. Tales of a great flood that nearly wipes out all life are among humanity's oldest recorded stories, dating at least from the second millennium B.C., and they appear in cultures from the Middle East to the Arctic Circle to the southernmost tip of South America and the islands of Polynesia. Typically gods are at the center of these ancient disaster tales—which is perhaps not too surprising, given the fact that the tales originated during a time when human beings were at the mercy of natural forces they did not understand.

To a great extent, we still are at the mercy of nature, as anyone who reads the newspapers or watches nightly news broadcasts can attest.

Hurricanes, earthquakes, tornados, wildfires, and floods continue to exact a heavy toll in suffering and death, despite our considerable knowledge of the workings of the physical world. If science has offered only limited protection from the consequences of natural disasters, it has in no way diminished our fascination with them. Perhaps that's because the scale and power of natural disasters force us as individuals to confront our relatively insignificant place in the physical world and remind us of the fragility and transience of our lives. Perhaps it's because we can imagine ourselves in the midst of dire circumstances and wonder how we would respond. Perhaps it's because disasters seem to bring out the best and worst instincts of humanity: altruism and selfishness, courage and cowardice, generosity and greed.

As one of the national chairmen of the American Red Cross, a humanitarian organization that provides relief for victims of disasters, I have had the privilege of seeing some of humanity's best instincts. I have witnessed communities pulling together in the face of trauma; I have seen thousands of people answer the call to help total strangers in their time of need.

Of course, helping victims after a tragedy is not the only way, or even the best way, to deal with disaster. In many cases planning and preparation can minimize damage and loss of life—or even avoid a disaster entirely. For, as history repeatedly shows, many disasters are caused not by nature but by human folly, shortsightedness, and unethical conduct. For example, when a land developer wanted to create a lake for his exclusive resort club in Pennsylvania's Allegheny Mountains in 1880, he ignored expert warnings and cut corners in reconstructing an earthen dam. On May 31, 1889, the dam gave way, unleashing 20 million tons of water on the towns below. The Johnstown Flood, the deadliest in American history, claimed more than 2,200 lives. Greed and negligence would figure prominently in the Triangle Shirtwaist Company fire in 1911. Deplorable conditions in the garment sweatshop, along with a failure to give any thought to the safety of workers, led to the tragic deaths of 146 persons. Technology outstripped wisdom only a year later, when the designers of the luxury liner *Titanic* smugly declared their state-of-the-art ship "unsinkable," seeing no need to provide lifeboat capacity for everyone onboard. On the night of April 14, 1912, more than 1,500 passengers and crew paid for this hubris with their lives after the ship collided with an iceberg and sank. But human catastrophes aren't always the unforeseen consequences of carelessness or folly. In the 1940s the leaders of Nazi Germany purposefully and systematically set out to exterminate all Jews, along with Gypsies, homosexuals, the mentally ill, and other so-called undesirables. More recently terrorists have targeted random members of society, blowing up airplanes and buildings in an effort to advance their political agendas.

The books in the GREAT DISASTERS: REFORMS AND RAMIFICATIONS series examine these and other famous disasters, natural and human made. They explain the causes of the disasters, describe in detail how events unfolded, and paint vivid portraits of the people caught up in dangerous circumstances. But these books are more than just accounts of what happened to whom and why. For they place the disasters in historical perspective, showing how people's attitudes and actions changed and detailing the steps society took in the wake of each calamity. And in the end, the most important lesson we can learn from any disaster—as well as the most fitting tribute to those who suffered and died—is how to avoid a repeat in the future.

LOVE CANAL
HOMEOWNERS ASSOC.
9905

Leader of the mission to expose the Love Canal, Lois Gibbs, talks with cancer research scientist, Beverly Paigan, just before an Environmental Protection Agency news conference. The EPA released its study showing that 11 of 36 Love Canal neighborhood residents had chromosomal damage.

1 A Mother's Crusade

In 1972, Lois Marie Gibbs moved into her new home on 101st Street in Niagara Falls. She was filled with all the hopes and joys of a new mother. The neighborhood she moved to was called the LaSalle Development. It was located on the southeast side of the city of Niagara Falls, not far from the grand Niagara River and its spectacular falls in western New York State. The population of Niagara Falls at the time was around 77,000, and the location was ideal as it was close to everything—stores, work, schools, Canada, and areas of historic interest.

The Gibbs family bought a small ranch house and owned two cars and a color TV. They were living the American dream. The neighborhood Lois and her husband, Harry, chose was quiet. The homes were well maintained and freshly painted. Yards were kept trimmed and

The Love Canal runs under the City of Niagara Falls, NY, which is named for the Niagara River and its mighty Falls. In the early 1900s, the Niagara River attracted companies that were eager to exploit the vast energy potential of the river and its Falls. The immense amount of water that runs through the Niagara River, and the Falls, is harnessed for hydroelectric power.

tidy and some of the streets were lined with trees. It was the perfect place to raise a family.

The Gibbs family chose this area not only because of the charming qualities the neighborhood possessed, but also because it gave them the convenience and attractions of city living without feeling like they were living downtown. Lois Gibbs liked the idea that her children would someday be able to walk to school, which was located on 99th Street. The playground was part of a big open field surrounded with homes. Neighbors had said the developers of the area were going to build a park on the field. This excited Lois. She often had visions of her family playing at the park, attending the school, and being an active part of the small neighborhood.

When the Gibbs bought their new home they were sure it was where they wanted to raise their family. Their young son, Michael, was born just before they moved in. Later in 1975 they had a daughter, Melissa. Life in their new neighborhood was everything they had expected it to be, until Michael turned six in 1978 and attended kindergarten at the school on 99th Street. For Lois, this is when the "Love Canal" saga began.

Lois Gibbs had no idea what the Love Canal was or where it was located. She had read some articles in the local *Niagara Gazette* about incidents of illnesses on some of the streets. It was known that toxic chemicals had been buried in the area, but no one seemed to pay much attention to this fact. The people who did complain lived on 99th and 97th Streets. Lois wrote in her book, *Love Canal: The Story Continues,* "I paid little attention. It didn't affect me, Lois Gibbs. I thought it was terrible, but I lived on the other side of Pine Avenue."

Lois was no different than so many of her neighbors. Unless she or her children were sick, the news didn't concern her. She had read some articles, heard the news, but felt like others in her neighborhood: it didn't affect her. Why should it? She lived several streets away. At the time, it hadn't even occurred to her that her son was attending the school on 99th Street—the very school that had been mentioned in the articles, and the same school that was located directly on top of the Love Canal.

Soon after Michael started kindergarten in September of 1978, he began having seizures. This confused Lois and her husband because seizures didn't run in their families. By December he had developed epilepsy; in February his white blood cell count had dropped. But how could this be? Leukemia didn't run in their families, either.

Lois knew that her son was sensitive to some medications and aspirin. She had been unable to give him aspirin as a baby. He would get sick to his stomach and break out in a rash. It also occurred to Lois that her son's school sat right on top of the Love Canal, the very place where toxic chemicals had been buried many years before. Was there a connection? If Michael was sensitive to medications, could he be sensitive to other chemicals? Lois wasn't sure, but she decided she had to find out. Watching their son suffer day after day with strange illnesses that seemed to materialize out of nowhere was more than Lois and her husband could bear.

The first thing Lois did was bring the articles to her brother-in-law, Wayne Hadley. He was a biologist and professor at the State University of New York at Buffalo. She asked him to explain what some of the words meant in the articles she had collected. She

Children in the Love Canal neighborhood attended school everyday at the school on top of a toxic waste dump. During recess, the kids played in the dirt contaminated with chemicals.

showed Wayne a list of chemicals that were known to be in the canal. What he told Lois shocked and upset her. Some of the chemicals could affect the nervous system and even a small amount could kill brain cells. Lois went to the *Gazette* and researched more articles. She couldn't believe what had been written about the area, the industry that once operated there, and what the company, Hooker Chemical Corporation, had done with the chemicals. Lois panicked. Thoughts of her son going to the school day after day frightened her. Her brother-in-law, Wayne, her husband, Harry, and Lois all agreed it was time to take him out of school.

Suddenly, the Gibbs' lives were turned upside down. Lois had a mission: to get her son out of the school, and every other child who attended the 99th Street School, as well. When Lois met with the superintendent of schools, she explained Michael's health problems to him: how Michael was sensitive to certain drugs and chemicals and that he was getting sick. She told him the school was sitting on top of a toxic waste dump site and Michael needed to be transferred. It was not safe or healthy for him or any child there to keep attending the school. Lois also stated that Michael could finish the school year but would not return the following year.

The superintendent told Lois she could not do that. In a word, a mother doesn't have the right to remove her child from school. He also told her she would need two doctors' statements. As ridiculous as it seemed to Lois, she went to Michael's pediatricians and got the statements she needed. She also talked to the doctors about the location of the school and the effects of toxic chemicals on children. The doctors didn't seem to mind giving Lois the statements that the superintendent required.

When Lois sent the doctors' statements to the superintendent, he did not respond. He wouldn't return her phone calls; when he finally did after a couple of weeks, he denied ever receiving the doctors' statements. But then he referred to the statements in his conversation. He told Lois that Michael could not be removed based on the statements, because the statements only alleged, they did not prove that the area was contaminated. How could he relocate all those children? Now it wasn't just Michael who needed to be removed, it was the entire school. Finally, the superintendent told Lois he did not believe the area was contaminated and he wasn't about to close the 99th Street School.

Shouldn't parents have the right to decide where their child goes to school? Lois Gibbs and her husband felt they had a right to make this decision but weren't sure how to go about it. Shouldn't children be able to attend school in a healthy, toxic-free, safe area? It was time to take action, serious action. Lois's mission had now become a crusade, not just for her child, but for all the children who attended the 99th Street School.

A Mother on a Mission

The very thought of going door-to-door scared Lois. She had never done anything like that before. She wondered what she would do if people were rude, or worse if they slammed a door in her face. What if her neighbors thought she was some crazy fanatic? How could Lois face them every day?

Lois prepared a petition that she would take around the neighborhood for signatures. The petition would show officials that the residents were concerned about their children attending the 99th Street School, and back up the notion that people in the area were getting sick. Feeling that she was on a mission, Lois tried to suppress all her fears. It was a warm, sunny day when she walked to 99th Street and Wheatfield Avenue and knocked on the first door. There was no answer. She stood there not knowing what to do. Instead of continuing to the next door, Lois gave up and went home.

It was time to face herself. Lois said, "When I got there, I sat at the kitchen table with my petition in my hand, thinking, Wait. What if people do slam the door in your face? People may think you're crazy. But what's more important—what people think or your child's health? Either you're going to do something or you're going to have to admit you're a coward and not do it." The next day Lois decided to talk with the people on her own street first. It would be easier to chat with them as she had always done. They were friends. They wouldn't slam the door in her face. The first person Lois spoke with was her son's best friend's father. Lois told him about the chemicals buried under the school and how worried she was about Michael's health. Then the father revealed that his son, Curtis, was hyperactive. The doctors had been telling him that it was all psychological. But now, he realized, maybe it had more to do with the chemicals than with anything else. The father signed the petition. With a renewed sense of confidence, Lois continued down her street, talking with neighbors and people she knew. She spent about 20 minutes with each person and discovered that people were concerned and wanted to know more about the Love Canal. Some didn't even know the canal existed. Lois spent much of her time educating her neighbors about the Love Canal, what it was, and its background. When people understood, they signed her petition. She also heard their stories about miscarriages, birth defects, and stillborn babies. These personal stories only backed up what Lois had originally feared: their neighborhood was killing them.

Support didn't always come so easily, especially in Lois's own home. Her mother thought she was crazy. The house was often messy, dinner sometimes late, which upset her husband. Harry, the kids, and the heat of the hot, humid summer were making Lois very tired. She said regardless of what others said or how she felt, something drove her on. She kept going door-to-door,

Lois Gibbs, a concerned neighborhood mother, made exposing the dangers of the Love Canal running under the neighborhood her personal mission.

not just on her own street but also on the next one and the next.

Finally she arrived at the homes on 99th Street. The first person she talked with was Mr. Frain. Lois told him she had a petition demanding the school be closed because their children's lives were in danger. He understood and signed the petition. He then showed her the steps on his front porch. They were separated from the porch by about two inches, as if the soil were sinking. He asked Lois if she could find out what was happening to his yard and home. Lois agreed but was unsure of what to do or whom to ask. As she continued down the street, she noticed there was a smell in the air. It was humid and the smell just hung there, thick and strong. Lois noticed her nose started to run and her eyes watered. She thought maybe it was psychosomatic —in other words, just thinking about the illnesses and toxic chemicals caused her to have symptoms. But knowing what kinds of chemicals lay under the ground and the danger they represented didn't stop Lois in her mission. She remembered her children, who were suffering the most, with the doctors' appointments, tests, and now her daughter, Melissa, was also terribly ill. She had developed saucer-sized bruises all over her body. The blood vessels beneath her skin burst. Her mouth and nose bled. Doctors performed a bone marrow test to see if Melissa might have developed leukemia. Not understanding why she needed tests, Melissa asked her mother what she had done wrong and why the doctors wanted to hurt her. Lois knew her children deserved better. She had to do whatever it would take to help her children and others like them to live the American dream in a safe, healthy environment. Going door-to-door was the least she could do, she decided; in time she would discover she would be tested in ways she couldn't have ever imagined.

The First Meeting

In June of 1978, the New York State Department of Health held a public meeting in the 99th Street School. It was one of the first meetings Lois attended. Dr. Nicholas Vianna and his staff explained they were performing environmental studies by taking samples of blood, air, and soil, and samples from sump pumps from the basements of some homes. (A sump is a low-lying pit or cesspool and a pump is used to remove the water.) They wanted to find out if there was really a problem. Neighbors filed into the auditorium and one by one gave accounts of things that were happening in their yards, neighborhoods, and homes. One lady mentioned how her dog's nose was burned when he sniffed the ground. Another man said when he put his daughter down in the backyard, the soles of her feet were burned. Lois had not heard these types of stories when she was out talking with neighbors. What did this mean? Were chemicals on the surface?

Dr. Vianna had no answers. While the residents sat in the stuffy auditorium, they grew more frustrated when they were told not to eat vegetables from their gardens. Lois asked him if the 99th Street School was safe. He answered that air readings taken at the school had come back clean. Meanwhile, Lois recalled, you could smell the chemicals hanging in the humid air.

In the weeks that followed, samples were taken. Lois continued her pursuit with the petition. She was meeting regularly with members of the New York State legislature as well as her brother-in-law, Wayne. Lois also talked with lawyers and initiated a lawsuit against the city and board of education of Niagara Falls, the county of Niagara Falls, and the Hooker Chemical Corporation, the company that allegedly dumped the chemicals in the Love Canal. Now people had another concern besides their health. Property values would be affected dramatically if the lovely neighborhood became known as a toxic waste site.

Lois continued to fight for her family and the health of others. She started the Love Canal Homeowners Association (LCHA) in 1978, which organized

More than 20 years after the Love Canal information surfaced, Lois Gibbs still works to fight environmental injustice. She heads the Center for Health, Environment, and Justice, an organization that helps neighborhoods recognize and get help for environmental contamination and its associated health problems.

the residents and gave them a spokesperson, Lois Gibbs. She became a nationally recognized spokesperson and political strategist for thousands of Niagara Falls residents. Lois continued to hold press conferences, negotiated with the governor, appeared on national television, testified before Congress, spoke at colleges, and so much more. Politicians who didn't seem to want to help and government agencies that were thoughtless and insensitive constantly confronted her. What kept Lois going, however, was that children were sick; some were dying. She watched men come to her office in tears, confused because they had nowhere to turn. One man walked in one day with tears streaming down his face. He told Lois that while he was watching TV, a bulldozer tore down his garage. His tools and things he had collected over the years were still in it. He asked Lois how the government could do that. He hadn't signed any papers selling his property to the government. They had no right. Lois agreed and made some phone calls. She got little sympathy. It was a mistake, they told her. But how do you explain this to someone whose garage was just bulldozed? Every day brought trials to Lois and the residents of the Love Canal. A mother on a crusade was faced with the unthinkable: a town in despair and wanting answers. To make matters worse, while she was trying to help others, her own family was suffering terribly. Not only were her two children ill and in need of seeing doctors but also Lois herself was exhausted and stressed. Many times she wanted to give up and walk away from her mission.

One of her biggest moments of despair was after a trip to Washington, D.C. The trip was exhausting, and she talked with people she had never met, trying to explain her situation. The trip home was hard. Her plane was diverted to Rochester and then she had to take a bus to Niagara. She was seated next to a drunken man who asked her where she had been. Lois told him and he soon recognized who she was, the woman at the Love Canal. He asked Lois if she was contaminated and jokingly, she replied, "Yes." The man wanted nothing more to do with her and wouldn't even put his arm on the rest. He stayed in the corner of his seat for fear of contamination. That's when it hit Lois. People were afraid of the residents at the Love Canal. Parents from other neighborhoods wouldn't let their kids play with the Love Canal kids or go anywhere near the Love Canal for fear of becoming ill.

When Lois finally got home she was hungry and tired. It was her son's birthday, and her daughter had made a cake. Lois ate it without even thinking. She had completely forgotten it was her son's birthday, something she had never done before. She hadn't even bought presents or planned a party. Michael was understandably upset, as was Lois. She was sacrificing her own normal life so others might have one. People were sick and she had to help them. She had to help her own children who had strange diseases and find a way for them to lead normal lives. It wasn't going to be easy, but a mother with a mission is hard to break.

Families were eventually relocated, including Lois and her family, and the once flourishing neighborhoods became ghost towns. Today, however, as a new century begins, people are moving back to the Love Canal area and starting to rebuild. Is it really safe? Many don't think so.

Lois has been criticized by many as being a grassroots activist who would stop at nothing to get her way. Some believe she used scare tactics and told half-truths. As with any story, there are two sides. Even today there is an ongoing debate about what really happened at the Love Canal, who was to blame and was it really the disaster so many people claim it to be. From the perspective of a concerned mother, Lois Gibbs, whose children were getting sick without an obvious reason, who faced a life of uncertainty, fighting back was the only way she knew to get answers and help. Hers was truly a mother's crusade, but not necessarily the entire story.

GRASSROOTS ACTIVIST

This term is often used when describing a group of people or a person—rather than a political party—actively involved in a cause at a local level. Lois Gibbs is called a grassroots activist because she initiated the investigation of the Love Canal site. She organized the neighbors and became their spokesperson. She set up picket lines and demonstrations to raise public awareness of the chemical peril that lay buried at the Love Canal site. Just as the roots of grass are at the bottom level of a grass plant, Lois Gibbs was at the bottom level of the crises at the Love Canal, thus the term "grassroots activist."

SOME OF THE MAIN PLAYERS IN THE LOVE CANAL SAGA

Lois Marie Gibbs: Mother and grassroots activist who became an outspoken representative for the residents of the Love Canal.

Dr. Paigen: Biologist, geneticist, and cancer research scientist at the Roswell Park Memorial Institute in Buffalo, New York. Worked closely with Lois Gibbs in determining whether or not the residents were being affected by the chemicals at the Love Canal. Worked on the swale theory.

Dr. Vianna: Worked for the Department of Environmental Conservation (DEC) and was first involved with the residents of the Love Canal. Worked with Lois on the swale theory, talked with residents, and did scientific studies at the Love Canal.

Dr. Whalen: Commissioner of the New York State Department of Health. Told the residents not to eat vegetables from their gardens and announced the closing of the 99th Street School.

Dr. Axelrod: Became the next commissioner of the New York State Department of Health after Dr. Whalen.

Congressman LaFalce: Congressman of New York who supported Lois Gibbs and the residents of the Love Canal.

The Niagara River caught the eye of William Love. Love wanted to connect the upper and lower parts of the river to create a man-made waterfall. The waterfall would have generated hydroelectric power.

Before the Love Canal Crises

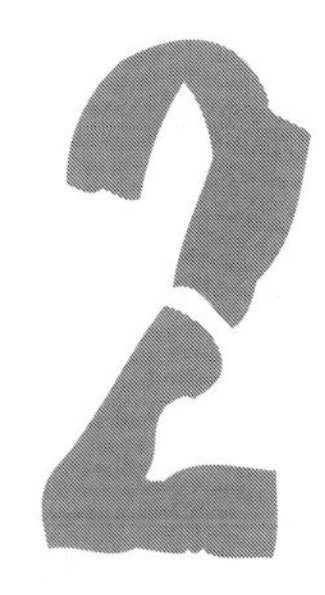

It is ironic that a place like the Love Canal would have a word such as *love* associated with it. Often when people hear the name, without knowing the truth of the Love Canal, visions of romantic gondola rides on a moonlit night come to mind: young couples gazing at the evening sky, sharing their hopes and dreams for a promising future as they float dreamily down the peaceful waterway. It is a *lovely* vision, but far from the realities and truths of the Love Canal that exists.

The Niagara River flows through this region. It is the same river that forms the beautiful and majestic Niagara Falls. The word *Niagara* is derived from an Indian word, *onguiaahra,* meaning "the straight." A more appropriate meaning of the word, "thunder of water," is also given. The river is strong and powerful. The noise is deafening as tons of water plunge below and the river continues on. As beautiful as they are to look at, one can't help but notice the power that the river and the falls generate. The Niagara Falls is considered one of the natural wonders of the world. They are a spectacular display of water and force. It is no surprise that early explorers and settlers noted not only the river's beauty but also its potential for water power. In 1759 Daniel Joncairs was the first recorded person to have harnessed a very small portion of the Niagara's power. He dug a narrow ditch above the falls on the American side and was able to draw enough water from the river to turn a waterwheel to power a small sawmill. Before his arrival, the Niagara River was used for washing clothes and transportation.

In 1805 Augustus and Peter Porter of Buffalo, New York, came to Niagara Falls. They purchased the American Falls from the state of New York at a public auction. With this purchase they acquired the water rights to the eastern rapids above and below the falls. The Porters built a water-powered gristmill and tannery along Joncairs's old ditch. The brothers were forced out of business when the Erie Canal opened 20 years later.

Stretching some 363 miles from the Hudson River at Albany to Lake Erie at Buffalo, New York, the Erie Canal was completed in 1825. The canal opened shipping lanes from the East Coast to the Great Lakes. Prior to the opening of the Erie Canal, goods and building supplies were shipped westward by horse-drawn wagons. The opening of the Canal enabled much larger payloads to be transported faster and at less cost.

There were no railroads in the United States and the Canal was the choice of transportation companies for the shipment of imported goods that were shipped up the Hudson River from New York City and the Port of New York. Albany, at the start of the Canal, quickly grew into a major transportation hub from which the western regions of New York State were developed. All along the Canal route, cities sprang up and industries were developed. This probably took business away from the Porter brothers, who had established themselves on the Niagara River, causing them to lose money and eventually go out of business.

The Porter brothers held on to the American Falls and their water rights. Augustus's initial plan was to use the power generated in the 50-foot (15 m) drop of the rapids above the falls, but he could not find interested financiers. Augustus dreamed of bigger and better things. He envisioned bypassing the falls with a hydraulic canal leading to a large reservoir on the cliff above the gorge. From there the water would flow to the base of the gorge to turbines connected by belts to industrial machinery above. Sadly, both brothers died before their vision became a reality.

In the 1830s engineers continued to recognize this area as a potential source of water power. When one considers the amount of horsepower driven by the water, it is understandable why people saw it as an inexpensive and easy way to produce energy. The average flow of water through the Niagara River equals 212,000 cubic feet of water per second, falling a distance of 325 feet from Lake Erie to Lake Ontario. This would yield a potential 8 million horsepower, or 5,965,600 kilowatts. (Horsepower is a unit of measure, a unit of power in the English system of units. It is equal to 33,000 foot-pounds per minute, or 550 foot-pounds per second, or approximately 746 watts. The term *horsepower* originated with James Watt, who determined by experiment that a horse could produce 33,000 foot-pounds of work a minute in drawing coal from a coal pit.)

Sawmills and flour mills were built along the Niagara River; but in 1848 something strange happened. In the early morning of March 29 of that year, the water in the

Hydroelectric power uses water flowing through a dam to spin turbines that generate electricity. Hydroelectric power uses natural processes to produce electricity cleanly.

upper Niagara River stopped flowing, bringing to a stop the mills operating from the power of the water. Only a trickle of water was finding its way down to the falls.

When the problem was investigated, a group of local men found an ice jam at the mouth of the Niagara River near Lake Erie. A severe winter and a northwesterly wind pushed the ice flow into the river. The phenomenon lasted for 40 hours. Only after a shift of wind to the east did the ice jam break up and the river and falls return to normal.

In 1853, just prior to the American Civil War, the Niagara Falls Hydraulic Power & Manufacturing Company was chartered. The Niagara Falls Hydraulic Power & Manufacturing Company had purchased the water rights, and in 1860, construction of the hydraulic canal began. The canal was 35 feet (11 m) wide and 8 feet (2.4 m) deep. It transported water from the Niagara River above the falls to the mill sites below. The canal construction was completed in 1861. Augustus Porter's vision became reality in 1875, when the wheels began turning in the new powerhouse.

With the use of water and wooden wheels, the movement activates a turbine that drives an electric generator. This process is called hydroelectric power generation. In more recent times the Niagara Falls and the Niagara River have been used to produce hydroelectric power. By 1881 the Niagara Falls Hydraulic Power & Manufacturing Company had built a small generating station and began providing electricity to light the village of Niagara Falls. It also provided power to several mills. This power plant became a tourist attraction. It operated a flour mill for two years before the company went bankrupt and all its assets were sold at public auction.

William T. Love proposed connecting the upper and lower Niagara River by digging a canal six to seven miles long so he could use the water of the upper Niagara River to create a man-made waterfall with a 280-foot drop that would provide greater and cheaper power. The year was 1892. This is where the Love Canal got its name. It has nothing to do with romantic notions and everything to do with money and business.

Shortly after Love's idea, the country fell into economic depression and Love lost all the backing he needed to fund his enterprise. As well, the invention of alternating electrical current made the transmission of electrical current over great distances possible, thereby eliminating the need for an on-site waterway to generate direct current power.

Abandoning the project, Love left a partially dug section of the canal. U.S. Geological Survey aerial photographs taken in 1927 show the section that had been dug was 3,000 feet long, 10 feet deep, and 60 feet wide, and was fed by creeks and streams stemming from the Niagara River. This trench was sometimes used for swimming, playing, and fishing by the local residents.

In 1920 the land was sold at a public auction and became a municipal and chemical disposal site. Elon Huntington Hooker developed the Hooker Chemical Company, located west of the canal. His plan was to turn the uncompleted canal into a dumping ground for the chemical by-products created by the company's manufacturing process. Burying waste was an acceptable way to get rid of by-products and was done by many companies. At this time, zoning regulations did not prevent waste disposal in and around neighborhoods and homes. In fact, people were generally unaware of the negative impact that such an industrial site might have on their health. Not much was known about the effects chemicals could have on the human body and the environment, and no one really seemed concerned.

Chemicals Found at Love Canal

Before the 1970s few people worried about chemical and hazardous waste. If it didn't affect them, they didn't think about it or how these dangerous materials were stored. Laws didn't exist to guide the process of getting rid of hazardous waste, and the easiest way for companies was to simply dump it anywhere.

The state health department's Division of Laboratories and Research has carried out more than 6,000 analyses of environmental and biological samples at the Love Canal since 1978. The Environmental Protection Agency (EPA) also made similar studies on the air, water, and soil. Their main interest was finding out what kinds of chemicals were at the Love Canal. Hooker Chemical also had to submit a declaration, which estimated that 21,800 tons of chemicals had been buried in the Love Canal over a period of 10 years. What were these chemicals and how were they buried? Many of the chemical names are words that are hard to pronounce and spell. Chemicals like thionyl chloride, trichlorophenol, and hexachlorocyclohexane were just a few named. All the chemicals were either liquid or solid and were buried in drums or nonmetallic containers.

It is important to understand the differences between *toxic* and *hazardous* chemicals. Toxic describes chemicals and substances that may cause death or serious injury to humans and animals. Hazardous is a broader term that describes all chemicals or chemical wastes that are dangerous to people or the environment. Household cleaners that end up in your trash can can be described as hazardous waste. The EPA identifies four categories of hazardous waste:

Corrosive—A corrosive material can wear away (corrode) or destroy a substance. For example, most acids are corrosives that can eat through metal, burn skin on contact, and give off vapors that burn the eyes.

Ignitable—An ignitable material can burst into flames easily. It poses a fire hazard, can irritate the skin, eyes, and lungs, and may give off harmful vapors. Gasoline, paint, and furniture polish are ignitable.

Reactive—A reactive material can explode or create poisonous gas when combined with other chemicals. For example, chlorine bleach and ammonia are reactive and create a poisonous gas when they come into contact with each other.

Toxic—Toxic materials or substances can poison people and other life forms. Toxic substances can cause illness and even death if swallowed or absorbed through the skin. Pesticides, weed killers, and many household cleaners are toxic.

Most toxic and hazardous materials come from industry.

During World War II, U.S. industry devoted its resources to producing weapons and other war material. A great example is the Manhattan Project. With the discovery of fission in 1939, it became clear to scientists that certain radioactive materials could be used to make a bomb of unprecedented power. U.S. president Franklin Delano Roosevelt responded by creating the Uranium Committee to investigate this possibility. Progress was slow until August 1942, when the project was placed under U.S. Army control and totally reorganized. The Manhattan Engineer District (MED) was the official name of the project. It is believed that some of the chemicals from this project were also dumped at the Love Canal site.

In laboratories scientists developed new chemicals and materials. Pesticides to kill weeds and insects were made stronger and our crop yields grew. Other research led to the development of plastics. We know today that plastics play a major role in our daily lives. Can you imagine life without plastic? Better quality paints, stronger detergents, and new fabrics like rayon and nylon

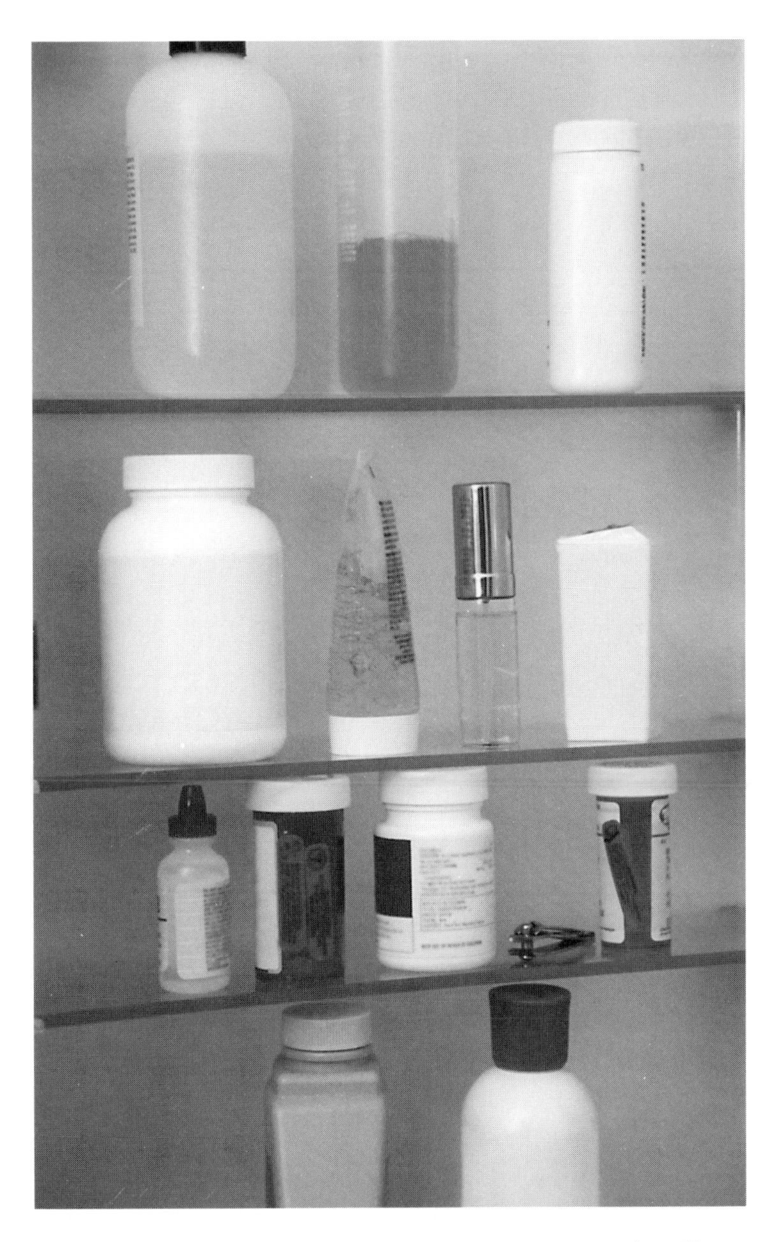

Chemical research, which often produces toxic byproducts, also produces many useful products. For example, scientists in chemical labs developed plastics. Today we use plastics on a daily basis in almost every facet of life.

were also developed, all with hazardous waste side effects. But our lives have been made easier and more convenient. Some people wonder at what cost. Because along with all these luxuries in life, there has been a price. That price is usually in the form of illness and the destruction of our environment, which takes years to fix.

Even Hooker Chemical had a good idea as to what kind of materials they were producing and how dangerous they could be. This was evident when they sold the land at a later date for one dollar and stated that people shouldn't live on the land. Today, there are strict guidelines on how to handle toxic chemicals and rules on wearing gloves, safety glasses, protective clothing, and masks to protect ourselves from the health dangers that exposure to such chemicals presents. If these chemicals are swallowed, they can be deadly. Children in particular, are more at risk for developing health problems when exposed to toxic chemicals—much as we saw at Love Canal.

Thousands of dump sites are found all over the United States. In the past, companies, as well as the military and federal government, disposed of chemical and hazardous waste by putting the material into metal drums. The drums were sealed and then buried in the ground.

Hooker Chemical, a subsidiary of Occidental Petroleum Corporation, is one such company that disposed of chemical waste by burying it. One of the largest chemical corporations in America, Hooker dumped 20,000–25,000 tons of toxic chemicals into the canal in metal drums from 1942 until 1953. However, they were not the only ones to do the dumping. The city of Niagara Falls, and the U.S. Army also used the site. The city dumped its garbage in the Love Canal site, and the army disposed of possible chemical warfare materials and parts related to the Manhattan Project there, as well. Hooker Chemical even dug the canal wider and deeper to make room for more hazardous material.

Hooker used electricity to turn brine into chlorine and caustic soda. Chlorine is a greenish yellow, poisonous gas with a disagreeable, suffocating odor; it is about two

EPA workers clean up dirt containing dioxin. In the Love Canal, tests showed low dioxin levels, but the EPA believes there is no safe level of dioxin. The workers must wear protective clothing because of the extreme toxicity of dioxin.

and one-half times as dense as air. Caustic soda is also known as sodium hydroxide. Sodium hydroxide is used primarily in the manufacture of other chemicals. It is also used in the manufacture of rayon and other textiles, paper, and soaps and detergents. Combined, sodium chloride and sodium hydroxide is used to bleach paper, and is an important component in the petroleum, pulp, and paper and aluminum industries.

Hooker Chemical put the hazardous materials in metal drums, buried them in the canal, and then covered

DIOXIN

Dioxin was eventually found in some areas of the Love Canal, although not in high numbers. Why are people afraid of dioxin, even in small amounts? Dioxin is one of the most toxic chemicals known to man. Even in small amounts, it is a health hazard. An EPA report states there is no safe level of dioxin, and it can cause severe reproductive and developmental problems in animals and humans. It also causes immune system damage and can interfere with hormone function. The presence of dioxin at the Love Canal site meant that the health threats at the site were not limited to children but included everyone in the area.

the canal with clay. The clay was expected to keep moisture away from the chemicals and act as a barrier, sealing the chemicals from contact with the environment. When the company had filled the site, it sold the canal and land to the local school board for one dollar.

As time went by and roads and houses were built on the land, heavy rains and snow caused the drums to leak. It was in 1958 that the first complaints began. The clay barrier once thought to protect the barrels was failing. Discolored, oozing soil was found in some basements and people began to complain. Investigators began to uncover barrels of toxic chemicals. In all, 400 different chemicals were eventually identified in the Love Canal.

Dioxin was one of these chemicals. It is actually a general term for a class of 75 chlorine-related compounds. Many scientists agree that dioxin in sufficient doses can cause cancer, skin problems, liver damage, and other illness—even death. It is no wonder that the residents of the Love Canal became increasingly worried about their health and lives.

Why is hazardous waste a problem? Eventually it finds its way into our drinking water, soil, and air. When enough toxic chemicals enter the human body, they can cause illnesses and even death. A key to our survival is an abundance of drinking water. But with contaminated groundwater, which is a major source of drinking water, we are seriously jeopardizing our future.

Although laws have been put into place since the Love Canal disaster, there are still problems. Landfills are poorly constructed; barrels are sealed improperly and still leak. Finding the space to deposit these drums is getting harder. Often they are dumped in the middle of the ocean. One has to wonder how much of our oceans is being contaminated by barrels lying deep beneath the sea.

Hooker Chemical has since moved from the Love Canal disaster, changing its name to Occidental. Many changes have also been made in the industry, and laws have been passed to protect the environment and citizens. The next question so many people have asked is, Why did the school board allow a school and eventually an entire community to be built on a known chemical waste dump? How did people begin to figure out the reason they were getting sick was because of where they lived? And who is to blame? The company that produced the chemicals and then buried them, or City of Niagara Falls, which knew the history of the canal and built on top of it anyway?

PAPER MILLS

Paper mills located on rivers and streams have been a leading producer of toxic and hazardous chemicals. The manufacture of paper requires great amounts of water, which eventually are released back into the environment as hazardous liquid waste. In a year an average paper mill may produce 8.2 billion gallons of liquid waste and emit 2 ounces of dioxin.

Breaking News

In 1953, Hooker Chemical Company buried metal drums filled with hazardous chemicals in the Love Canal. The mounds of dirt used to cover the toxic chemicals would later become the contaminated dirt of the 99th Street School playground.

After World War II there was a huge economic boom in the United States. People were happy; the war had been won and now it was time to resume the good life in America. People married and had babies, new homes and communities were being built, and it seemed things were going on as before, only better because people were working, producing, and making more money.

The Hooker Chemical Company in the City of Niagara Falls was no different. It was growing, with sales in the millions of dollars by the 1950s. By 1953 Hooker had dumped so many chemical-filled metal drums in Love Canal, that they found themselves with no more room to dump their waste. The time had come to cover the Canal and move on.

Love Canal, with its 21,000 tons of toxic chemicals (which equals about

42 million pounds), was covered with dirt and the final layer with clay. It's hard to believe that thousands of barrels lay just below the surface of what was once a huge canal that ran through the area. Sixteen acres of dirt sat unused. Hooker Chemical decided to sell the land. They sold it to the City of Niagara Falls Board of Education for one dollar. Nowhere in America could anyone buy 16 acres of land for a dollar, but this land came with a warning. In the transfer of deeds, Hooker Chemical made it clear that there were toxic chemicals buried beneath the ground, which could pose a health hazard. Hooker Chemical thought that such a disclaimer would protect them from any liability. They were wrong.

In 1954, America continued to prosper, and so, too, did the City of Niagara Falls. To meet the need for more schools and housing, the City and the board of education decided to expand the housing community on and around the Love Canal site. They also built a school directly on top of the landfill. This school was named the 99th Street Elementary School. When people began purchasing these homes, they were not warned about the dangers under their homes. When they sent their children to school, they were not told that the school was built on top of toxic chemicals. Four hundred children attended the school and played on the playground. The school was often a common meeting place for families after school and on weekends. But no one knew what lurked below.

In the 1960s there was another housing boom and more homes were built around the Love Canal. As new houses continued to go up, some residents began complaining about a black, oily substance in their basements, sump pumps, and backyards, as well as an odor. Some of these complaints were filed and city officials would come out to check the area, but little was actually done to address the problems.

In some instances, the city covered the substances over with more dirt, including some found on the school property. As complaints continued, Calspan Corporation was eventually hired to investigate. They filed a report saying there was toxic chemical residue in the air and in the sump pumps in residents' homes located on the southern end of the canal. They also discovered that 50 gallon drums had resurfaced to just below the clay cap. High levels of PCBs (polychlorinated biphenyls) were discovered in the storm sewer system. Although PCBs are no longer manufactured in the United States, their long degradation time ensures that they will be an environmental nuisance and health hazard for years to come. Remedial recommendations included covering the canal with a clay cap, sealing home sump pumps, and installing a tile drainage system to control migration of wastes. Action should have been taken, but it wasn't.

In the early 1970s the last of the houses went up in the area. Lois Gibbs was a buyer of one of these houses in 1972. She and her husband had no idea what they were buying into. No one told them about the chemicals, the hazards, and the complaints. By 1976, however, the news coverage about Love Canal began to heat up, and Lois soon realized she was sitting on a time bomb.

News about Love Canal made headlines in the *Niagara Gazette*. According to a timeline put together by the *Gazette,* on October 3, 1976, the paper reported that materials from a chemical landfill between 97th and 99th Streets were seeping into basements of homes in the area. There were also reports of illnesses and injury to animals. On November 2, 1976, the *Gazette* reported that the chemical analyses of residues near the old Love Canal dump site indicated the presence of 15 organic chemicals, including three toxic chlorinated hydrocarbons. On

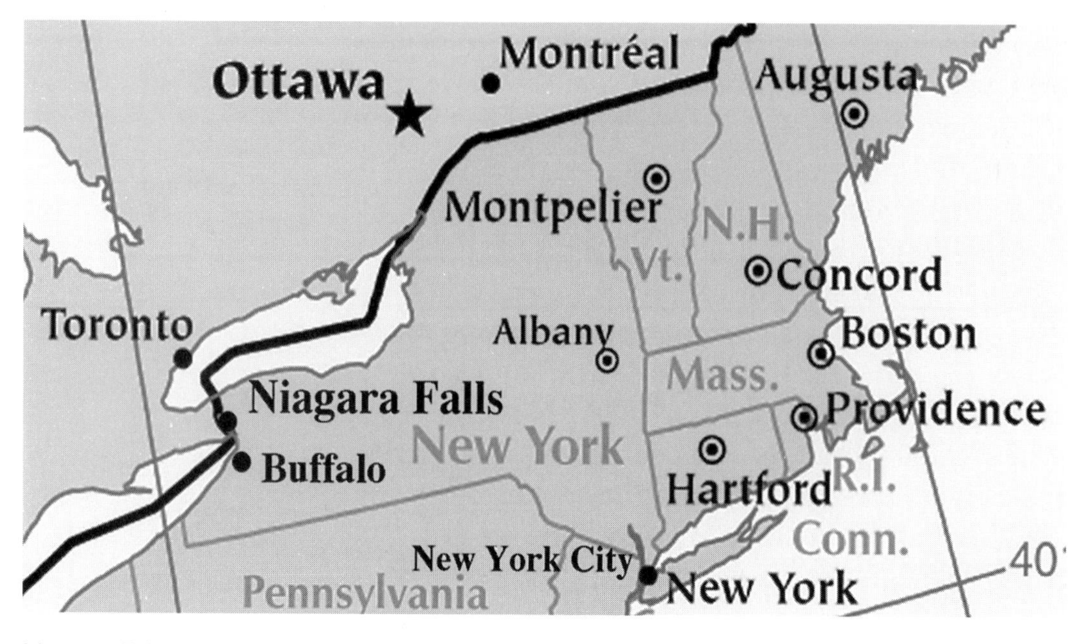

Niagara Falls and the City of Niagara Falls is on the border of the United States and Canada in the State of New York.

November 4, 1976, the *Gazette* reported that toxic chemicals were seeping into basements and sump pumps. The chemicals were then carried via the water through storm sewers and dumped into the Niagara River. Complaints of odors and strange substances continued.

October 8, 1977, the EPA, brought in by Congressman John LaFalce, issued a report on its alarming findings. They discovered that a landfill did exist and that barrels containing hazardous and toxic materials were rusting. Where the barrels had sunken and started to deteriorate, there were empty holes, that looked like potholes. Sometimes topsoil, water, and waste filled these holes. Some holes oozed continuously, and water and waste accumulated in basements and yards of certain homes. The color of the water that filled the potholes changed at different times. Chemical odors were prevalent in the landfill area and basements of some homes. The odor penetrated clothing even after it was washed. The sump pumps in some homes had an odor and were also covered with an oily film. Seepage into some basements had rotted wood partitions and attacked paint on basement walls.

The New York State Department of Environmental Control had previously conducted some studies, but they came up inconclusive, according to an earlier EPA report. But the EPA report did conclude that unhealthy and hazardous conditions existed at the site of the landfill and some surrounding homes. Surface drainage was poor, and instead of water going over the site, as it was originally planned, water went through it. Unknown chemicals permeated the site, and the condition of the barrels was unsatisfactory.

The city, the New York State Department of Conservation, and Congressman LaFalce all stated that they wanted to help the people. Correcting the problems at the Love Canal would take many years, and a temporary solution wouldn't work. It had to be permanent. Families would have to be relocated, and even then it might be years before they could receive all the relief they needed. The site must be cleaned completely and thoroughly.

The report also stated that it did not know who was to blame. Questions were brought up about Hooker's responsibility, as well as the city's responsibility in the whole mess. Hooker denied any responsibility or wrongdoing, as they had warned the city and school board at the time of the sale of the land that hazardous waste was buried at the Love Canal site.

Cleaning up a hazardous waste site is complicated, costly, and time consuming. The EPA recommended that all chemicals and chemically infected soil and debris be removed. Then the area should be filled in with new, clean dirt. The land would have to be regraded to assure proper drainage.

The final conclusion from the EPA report was grim. They saw no immediate relief for the residents except to relocate some of them. The problem would never be corrected unless all the dirt and debris were removed and groundwater flow was directed away from homes. Then maybe, just maybe it would be safe for people to return to the Love Canal neighborhoods and resume their lives.

In April of 1978, Michael Brown, a reporter from the *Niagara Gazette,* began running more articles about the Love Canal, and the report by the EPA was made public. Residents were starting to take it seriously. They called for more tests. At the same time the New York State Department of Health began collecting air and soil samples from basements and conducting health studies of the 239 families immediately surrounding the canal. On April 25, 1978, the New York State commissioner of health, Dr. Robert Whalen, issued a determination of public health hazard existing in the Love Canal community. He ordered the Niagara County Health Department to remove exposed chemicals from the site and install a protective fence around the area.

The report was not good news to Lois Gibbs. How can you relocate so many people? And the number of people being considered was only a small portion of the people who were affected. By 1978 there were 800 private single-family homes, 240 low-income apartments, and the 99th Street Elementary School. Residents became more concerned and started to keep track of their own health problems. On August 2, 1978, Robert Whalen declared a medical emergency at the Love Canal and ordered the 99th Street School to be closed. He also warned people not to go into their basements, clean their yards, or eat food from their gardens.

On August 4 of that year, residents formed the Love Canal Housing Association (LCHA) and elected Lois Gibbs as president. Gibbs set up goals for the association:

Newspapers picked up the story of the Love Canal residents and took the issue to the national consciousness. Having a nationwide audience would help the residents get federal help to move out of their neighborhood.

(1) get all residents who want to be evacuated, evacuated or relocated; (2) protect the values of their homes; (3) get the canal fixed properly; and (4) have air and soil sampling done in the entire area.

Other organizations were also established to help the Love Canal residents. Local churches formed the Ecumenical Task Force, with Sister Margeen Hoffman as executive director. Eventually, as the crises continued, these groups helped families find temporary housing, food, clothing, and transportation.

On August 7, 1978, Jimmy Carter, president of the United States, declared the Love Canal area a federal emergency. This was the first time that the nation had declared an environmental disaster. The designation meant the funds needed to relocate the 239 families living in the first two rows of homes encircling the landfill could be taken care of and the clean-up process could begin. The federal government agreed to give New York $20

The children in the Love Canal area ran a particularly high risk of health problems. Authorities urged families to move their children from the contaminated area, and also urged pregnant women to relocate. The problem: these families had no one to buy their property and had nowhere to go.

million to buy the homes of people who lived within two blocks of the canal.

Lois Gibbs was happy for the residents of that area, but not for her own family and the residents who lived near her. They were not affected by this declaration. By helping to form the LCHA, she soon realized the residents must come together in an orderly fashion. Town meetings, where people could speak their minds, were getting them nowhere. Confusion reigned at the meetings, and the more people talked, the greater their fear. The LCHA became the voice of the residents, and because Lois was the president, she did most of the talking.

Still, articles continued to appear throughout the month of August 1978 and thereafter. Headlines stated: "Evacuation of Kids Urged," "State to Assume Canal Mortgages," and "Canal Aid Phone Numbers." In an article written by Michael Brown entitled, "Evacuation of Kids Urged," he said two of the known pregnant women in the area would be temporarily relocated, and that about 20 families with children under the age of two should also leave. He went on to say no state funds were made available to help these people move.

The news worsened as a report surfaced of 200 tons of lethal dioxin buried in the canal. This report was issued on November 10, 1978. On November 22, over 200 chemical compounds were identified as being buried in the canal. The residents' fears and concerns heightened. The state refused to relocate 54 families who resided on the outskirts of the contaminated area. Residents protested, and seven homeowners were arrested, although the charges were later dropped. Parents were most worried about their children, and their worries were confirmed when, on January 23, 1979, Dr. Beverly Paigen, a cancer researcher at Roswell Park Memorial Institute in Buffalo, publicized her study. It showed a high rate of birth defects and miscarriages among the Love Canal families. She also found that children in the area had higher-than-normal rates of learning disabilities, seizure disorders, eye and skin irritations, and severe stomach pains. These studies were disturbing to the residents, yet they already knew that something was seriously wrong. They watched their children suffer, some with strange diseases and symptoms. They felt helpless and trapped and wondered what they could do to save their children.

Children at Risk

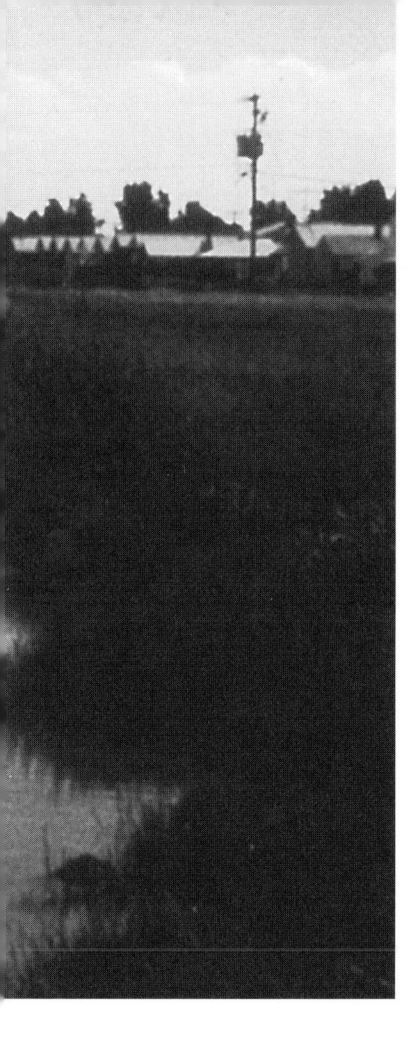

Glowing pools of contaminated liquid rose to the surface of the playground of the 99th Street School in 1978.

"Twenty years ago, when the public first heard the words *Love Canal,* I was a young mother living in the City of Niagara Falls, New York, just three blocks east of the Love Canal dump site, which contained 20,000 tons of more than 200 different chemicals. I set out to investigate whether my neighbors' children were as sick as my children were. As I went door-to-door, I was shocked to hear stories of birth defects, miscarriages, cancers, and the leaking of multicolored chemical ooze into basements. My fears were confirmed—our families were at risk."

Over the course of the next 10 years or so, Lois Gibbs would be a witness to countless tragedies within the families who resided on and around the Love Canal. What she heard made her angry and determined to help these people. What she saw firsthand broke her heart. The people who suffered the most were also the most innocent, the children. Not only did many suffer physical ailments but also the stress and fear of thinking they could get sick or might even die caused a tremendous amount of anxiety. Because of this anxiety and stress, families were torn apart. Marriages broke down as couples became unable to cope with all the bad news and the hard decisions. Children were sent to homes of other family members or friends to keep them away from the toxic chemicals believed to be causing the illnesses. The children of the Love Canal were afraid. What would a six year old think if he couldn't go to school anymore because it was closed down? How would an eight year old feel if she couldn't run barefoot on a hot summer day? How do you tell your ten year old he can't live at home anymore because it is too dangerous? How does a mother like Lois Gibbs and so many others explain to her children, test after test, needle after needle, that the doctor is really trying to help them so they don't get sick? And what is a dioxin, anyway? Foreign words, big and scary, all seem to mean the same thing: danger!

A mother named Anne Hillis was one parent who watched her children suffer. In a report to a Senate committee in April 1979 she explained her family's situation. She had lived at the Love Canal for 13 years, but since the discovery of toxic chemicals everything had changed. She said, "I hate my life at Love Canal. It's a strange life that I lead now, it is filled with disruptions, frustrations, sleepless nights, and a grip of fear that only those in similar situations can understand."

In her testimony, Hillis described the situation with her son, who was 10 years old at the time. He attended the 99th Street School. He did well at the school but had always had health problems, starting in kindergarten when he became very ill. He was diagnosed with acute

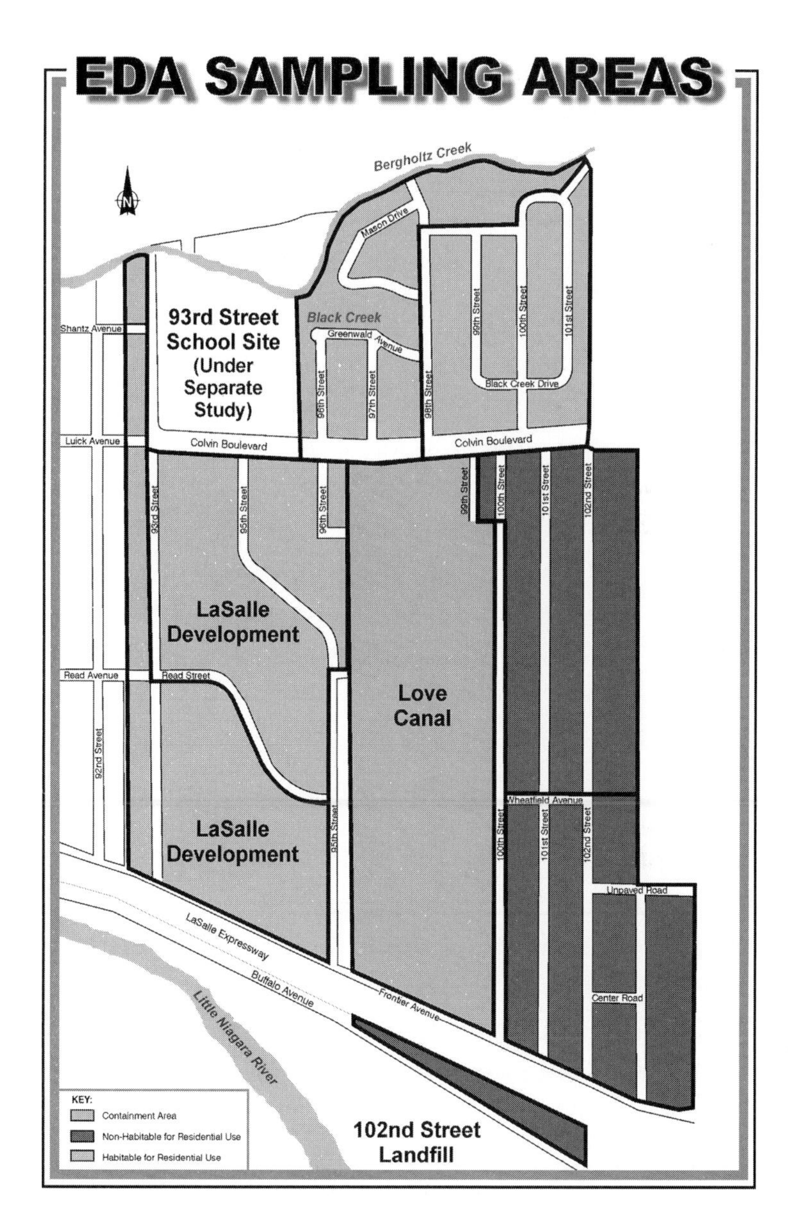

This map shows the position of Lois Gibbs' neighborhood, the 99th Street School, and the Love Canal waste dump.

gastroenteritis. At age 6 he developed tonsillitis and had his tonsils and adenoids removed. He suffered a respiratory infection that did not improve and he eventually developed asthma. At age 8 he had to see an allergist. When the 99th Street School was closed, he was sent to another school miles away. He started his first year there with an abscess in his nose, repeated respiratory infections, and asthma.

The final straw for Hillis came when she found her son at two in the morning on a cold winter night hiding under a couch, crying. When Hillis asked him what was wrong, he replied, "I want to die, I don't want to live here anymore—I know you will be sick again and I'll be sick again."

Disease and birth defects have been on the rise around the world, not only at Love Canal. As countries and companies produce more products, more waste is produced. Some countries don't have the same strict laws and regulations that we now have here in America since the events at Love Canal occurred. So how do we know if our bananas, which are imported from other countries, are safe to eat? The use of pesticides alone to control disease and insects in plants has increased over the years. Unless you thoroughly wash the produce you buy, chemical residue remains on it, therefore when you eat produce, you likely ingest some of this residue. When you breathe molecules of chemicals carried in the air enter your body. Drink water and eat fish and you might also ingest some hazardous and toxic chemicals. Now these amounts are usually pretty low and won't harm you, at least as far as we know. Today, studies are being conducted on the long-term effects from these chemicals.

In the 1960s and '70s residents of Love Canal had no idea they were being exposed to chemicals in all these ways. They were told in 1978 not to grow or eat vegetables from their gardens. Chemicals in the soil would find their way into the vegetables. Maybe the water wasn't safe to drink either because the water going into and out of homes ran through the dump site deep in the ground. Better to buy bottled water, as Lois Gibbs ended up doing. And the awful smell that seemed to linger in the air was of chemicals being blown either from the chemical plants along the river or seeping up through the ground in the form of gas. But before news got out in the mid-1970s, there was unknown danger in the ground. Residents at the Love Canal lived normal lives, thinking they were safe.

Still, the question remains, how do we protect ourselves and, especially, our children, who are so at risk to the harmful effects of chemical exposure? Children, because of their small stature, live closer to the ground than adults; therefore, they are more likely to come in contact with chemicals and hazardous waste. Their behavior, diet, and activities make children easier targets for chemicals. Many felt this described what was happening at the Love Canal and why so many children were suffering.

Children are not little adults. This means much of their body hasn't developed or is in the process of developing. It is believed children come into greater contact with dangerous chemicals because they eat more than adults in proportion to their body weight. These chemicals include the pesticide residues on fruits and vegetables and in juices. The EPA classifies as possible carcinogens over 65 percent of the 560 million pounds of herbicides and fungicides sprayed annually on U.S. crops. The average child consumes four times the amount of these suspect chemicals than adults. This is a scary thought when we realize how we push children to eat as many fruits and vegetables as possible. Although the vitamins provided by the fruit or vegetable are healthy for the human body, the pesticides with which they are treated are not.

The digestive system in children is immature. Children can absorb 50 percent of the lead they accidentally ingest, whereas adults will absorb only 10 percent. In children it will take 10 months for the lead to be

Children have a higher risk of contamination because they are small and therefore closer to the ground. Children are much more likely to have repeated contact with the ground, inhaling and ingesting chemicals as they play in the dirt.

absorbed, whereas in an adult, only 1 month. The study of lead poisoning in children has given us many answers for curing lead poisoning. The only true cure is to get rid of lead in the environment altogether. But the study of pesticides and the effects they have on children has been slow. Many believe pesticides can do as much damage, if not more, to children as lead.

When a child is developing in his early years he is more susceptible to health problems, especially if he is exposed to hazardous and toxic materials. A baby in the womb or newly born is most at risk. Some studies at Love Canal have indicated that birth defects there were higher and birth weights lower than normal. This seemed especially true around wetland areas. Lois Gibbs came up with a theory she called the swale theory. She outlines this theory in her book, *The Love Canal: The Story Continues.* Lois drew a map of the swales around the Love Canal area. A swale is a low-lying and often wet stretch of land. Along with the help of some residents, she conducted a survey to see what kind of illnesses existed in different areas. Her survey showed that along these swales, birth defects, low birth weights, and miscarriages were higher than normal. Why? Perhaps in these areas the toxic chemicals that were buried weren't far enough below the surface, thereby allowing gaseous fumes to rise more easily than those from chemicals buried much deeper in the ground. Water would erode metal barrels over time and also carry chemicals to the water supplies.

Lois said, "I was surprised: the illnesses clustered along the swales. I had very little data at this time, but the central nervous system and neurological problems, the migraines, epilepsy, and hyperactivity followed the swale. The birth defects made a perfectly straight line. . . . The birth defects were in houses that stood back-to-back. It looked like every house on a corner or near one had a child with a birth defect." Although the survey certainly seemed to show that there was a common link between low-lying ground and wetlands and birth defects, admittedly the survey wasn't scientifically accurate. To determine if there was a link, the New York State Department of Health conducted its own studies.

In order to have reliable results, a study must include control groups. A group of people in an affected area is studied against another group of people in a non-affected area. Compared to the non-affected control group, it did appear that birth defects and low birth weights occurred more often in the swale areas around the Love Canal. Some children in these areas never had a chance.

In March 2000, the New York State Department of Health posted a newsletter at its website. It was a follow-up health study. The department realized, too, that children, because they play outdoors near the canal, would be more likely than adults to be exposed to chemicals. It asked residents to write to the department and tell about their childhood experiences. Their stories are shocking. But remember, they simply had no idea how hazardous the playground was.

The Love Canal children were just like any other children in America. They enjoyed the same activities and found ample places and room to play. This included swimming in the canal, biking on the canal banks and across the field, throwing "fire rocks" at the canal, building forts near the canal, playing baseball, kick ball, football on the canal field (the 99th Street School, which, you'll remember, was built on top of the canal, also had a large field). Other activities included playing tag, hide-and-seek, sledding down the canal banks, and skating on the canal. Yet here, all the normal everyday childhood activities were potentially lethal.

One long-time resident of the Love Canal area wrote that, between 1933–1950, as a teenager, he used to swim in the canal with family and friends. He also recalled running home to hose off a brown-colored coating that covered his body.

Another resident wrote that, between the years 1942–1954, "When they were dumping, I used to play on

the steam shovel and other equipment after they were done working. We played in the hole they dug and on top of the barrels. Sometimes the fumes were so bad we had to leave."

And yet another resident, recalling the years between 1967–1978, wrote, "I was one of the kids . . . that played during the day and hung out every night either at the school or in the fields. I still remember the colored puddles and dirt we rode our bicycles and motorcycles on. We dug and played in it just like you'd expect kids to do. I still remember the smell on my clothes."

Not only did children play on the Love Canal but

The children of Love Canal were like any other. They spent their days playing games or building forts outside. The difference is that fumes, contaminated water, and strange puddles colored their world.

The Love Canal area went from being a thriving neighborhood of playful children and cordial neighbors to a barren shell of a community.

Scared of what the future might hold for them, however, the residents of the affected area decide not to wait for government bureaucracy to determine their fate, and, instead do whatever it takes to make themselves heard.

The Great Escape

Many people boarded up their homes and found any way to leave the Love Canal area. The first "great escape" occurred in 1978, the second occurred two years later.

5

In fact, there were two "escapes" that took place around the Love Canal area. The first was in 1978. The second followed a few years later, in 1980. In less than a week's time, between August 2 and August 7 of 1978, the state health commissioner declared a state of emergency at the Love Canal and ordered the closing of the 99th Street Elementary School. Pregnant women and children under the age of two were asked to go elsewhere, away from the Love Canal and its contaminated air, soil, and water. On August 7, the president of the United States, Jimmy Carter, approved federal financial aid for the area so New York could start buying the homes of the 239 families who lived in the first two rings surrounding the 99th Street Elementary School. The relocation process cost $10 million. Families didn't know where to go. Some stayed with relatives, others in motels.

As Lois Gibbs writes in her book, *Love Canal: The Story Continues,* the process was complicated and never went as easily as it could have. On August 8, she reports, state officials decided they would move only Ring 1 families, not those in Ring 2. People were upset. The homes in Ring 2 had also tested positively and those families wanted out! Eventually Ring 2 also was relocated, and by January 1979, almost all the families of Rings 1 and 2 had been relocated. The state signed 232 purchase agreements, and to further assist these residents, it provided $1.2 million for a support program. Of this money, $200,000 would be used to contract with the United Way of Niagara Falls to provide psychological and family counseling for area residents.

On November 10, 1978, it was reported that 200 tons of the lethal chemical dioxin had been buried in the canal. There seemed to be more of an urgency to relocate Rings 1 and 2. The process of relocating this many people in such a short amount of time was intense. People were brought in by the state to help with the process. Buying and selling a single home is difficult enough, and dealing with over 200 homes and their families in a short amount of time is unprecedented. The state allowed the residents choices. They decided where they wanted to be relocated. Their homes were bought at existing fair market value, though many residents complained the economy was experiencing a depression and so they received far less for their homes than what the homes were worth. Houses had to be appraised to determine their fair market value, families needed help in finding places to rent or buy, an inventory had to be taken of the homes the state bought, and families needed help in moving. The American Red Cross, the Salvation Army, and the United Way also helped residents with their relocation plans.

Although many of the residents living near the Love Canal site were relocated, the residents living outside of Ring 1 and Ring 2 were not, and they were not happy. Lois Gibbs was one of those people. There were families living outside the two rings that had poor health records and their homes were contaminated. Some households had pregnant women or small children. The United Way temporarily relocated these families. They lived in a hotel, which wasn't easy with children. Where do you cook your food? Do your laundry? Residents of the area were getting excited, though, because they felt the state was finally going to help them too. Most families wanted to be relocated. About 30 families between 97th and 103rd Streets had to be relocated soon because of pregnant women or young children living in the homes. They were the most vulnerable to chemical fumes and contamination. It seemed for a moment it would happen. Testing continued in homes as well as on residents. More homes outside the original first two rings were testing positive for chemical contamination. Finally, notice was given that the decision as to whether the remaining residents would be relocated would be made at some future date.

The United Way, which was supporting families living in hotels and in other services, had run out of money. As the families waited to hear about future relocation plans, they were forced to leave the hotel and move back to their contaminated homes. The day Lois received the news, reporters and residents gathered outside her office. The news came: relocation had been denied.

All the families outside the two designated rings had been denied relocation. The reason was not related to the question of contamination but rather to the likelihood of the canal spontaneously combusting—i.e., igniting. Sometimes in chemical dumps, the chemicals react in such a way that they begin to burn, sometimes even exploding. As the state decided that there was no risk of the canal exploding, the residents could return to their homes. Many tears were shed, and the families felt abandoned. They had seen the state's decision regarding relocation as their last chance to get out of the Love Canal and regain their health. They were left without hope. Some women were pregnant; others had young children. They couldn't go back to the Love Canal, but what could they do?

Lois Gibbs was desperate. Day after day families visited her office, fearful of what might happen to them. She was afraid for her own family too. Frustrated with the state government, Lois Gibbs fought back, but not in conventional ways. She tried to have Commissioner Whalen arrested for child abuse. He was part of the group that denied the residents relocation, and Lois felt he was endangering the lives of children. It didn't work. Residents continued to form picket lines in the area, but Lois found other outlets: television, for example. She appeared on the *Phil Donahue Show* and stated she would "blast Governor Carey on television." She made this threat in hopes that Governor Carey would take more action in helping the residents of the Love Canal. As Lois points out in her book, the interview on the show was a disaster. A Dr. Epstein who had written the book, *Politics of Cancer,* was also on the show, and he basically stole the spotlight from Lois. She returned from her trip to Chicago ready to warn residents and her family of the doomed interview on the show.

Lois soon realized her biggest problem would be keeping the media interested in the residents' plight. She appeared on other television shows and broadcasts. She also organized some residents to take a child's and

Tim Moriarty, a Love Canal resident, voices his anger at the situation. Moriarty lived in the neighborhood for 35 years. The state government decided to deny Moriarty's request for relocation because they determined that the Love Canal situation presented no danger to him and other residents in the surrounding area.

an adult's coffin to the state capitol in Albany and give them to Governor Carey. This was a bold statement on the part of the residents of the Love Canal. But, according to Lois, the media in Albany didn't understand their situation and had little sympathy. They asked, "Why don't you just move?"

Lois explained that when you bring home only $150 a week, have a house payment, doctors' bills, and other debts to pay, when you can't even sell your home because no one would want to buy it—how do you just move? It was much easier said than done, and after all, Love Canal was their home and, for some residents, had been their home for many years.

1979 and early 1980 were a roller coaster ride for Lois Gibbs and the residents of the Love Canal. Lois was gaining national recognition. She spoke in front of Congress, met the president, and had celebrities such as actress Jane Fonda join her cause. A bill to help the residents at the Love Canal went before the state legislature and passed. It finally looked like all the residents would be relocated, but when? There were still no plans as to when all this would occur. Residents were happy; finally something would be done—or would it.

On May 19, 1980, a shocking announcement hit the headlines: "White House Blocks Love Canal Evacuations." Over a hundred residents gathered at the LCHA office, crying and angry. Some lit fires on the lawn across the street. Lois reported in her book, "My reverie of feeling sorry for myself was interrupted when I heard one of the residents saying we should take the EPA representatives hostage. 'Let's see how much they like being in this neighborhood. If we can't leave and we have to die here, then they can too!'"

Soon after two EPA representatives showed up, Lois took them hostage. She called the White House, but to no avail. The hostages were treated well and served homemade food. They also had full use of the phone. The crowd outside continued to grow, and Lois became fearful for her hostages' lives. She couldn't release them into the angry crowd. Now she became their protector, but she still referred to them as her

Tony Manganero, carrying his TV out of the house, leaves the Love Canal neighborhood. Manganero and other residents moved into temporary housing to get their families out of the toxic area.

"hostages." Her attorneys called and warned if she kept calling them hostages, she could land in prison for five years. Lois didn't care. They didn't understand how desperate the residents were. Finally the FBI called and demanded Lois release the EPA representatives, and she was given seven minutes to do so. As the FBI counted down the minutes over the phone, Lois went outside to calm the residents. When the EPA officials were finally released, Lois and the other Love Canal residents went home. Some called Lois a traitor for releasing the EPA officials; others were happy with her decision.

Jimmy Carter signed a bill allocating $20 million to residents of the Love Canal area to aid in their relocation. Although the officials insisted that the health problems did not exist, Carter signed the bill to ease the mental anguish of the Love Canal residents.

On May 21, 1980, the actions of Lois Gibbs and the residents of the Love Canal seemed to pay off. President Carter declared the Love Canal a national emergency and that 710 families would be relocated. Television and radio stations covered the event. Champagne was brought in to help celebrate at the LCHA office. Lois said, "People were laughing, crying, hugging each other, dancing around and saying, 'We won! We won!'" They all felt they were free from the Love Canal and their children and babies were finally safe.

The following days saw a parade of area residents go to local hotels, motels, and apartments. The following months were equally confusing and busy. Lois Gibbs appeared on numerous television shows, including the

Phil Donahue Show again and *Good Morning America*. She rallied support from people all over the nation. Concerned citizens wrote letters to the White House, and Lois believes this greatly helped in the Love Canal residents' cause. Soon, President Jimmy Carter paid a visit to Love Canal. After his speech, he invited Lois Gibbs to join him on the stage. She did and she also told him what the residents of the Love Canal needed to make their relocation easier and complete. They simply didn't have the money to buy new homes. A revitalization committee was established and given $20 million to help the families relocate. The committee offered tax breaks and low-interest loans to residents. Gibbs said President Carter signed the bill for this revitalization committee because of the residents' mental anguish and not because federal officials agreed there was a health hazard at the Love Canal. And in that lies the big question.

Was there truly a health hazard at the Love Canal? It is still being debated today. Most of the residents living at the Love Canal felt their lives were in danger. Some scientists and health officials disagreed. The debate over the 1980 relocation of residents still goes on, and the answers may not be known for a long time.

Scientists conducted test after test to determine the exact levels of toxicity in the Love Canal. Despite their findings, some insisted that living on the Love Canal was not dangerous.

The Great Debate

As with any story, there are two sides, two points of view, and two ways of thinking. And so it is with the Love Canal story. On one side you have concerned mothers and fathers living in an area known to have been a toxic waste dumping ground. There is no denying the smells that permeated the air and people's homes, the ooze seeping into basements, or the colorful puddles that never seemed to go away on the playground. The residents of the Love Canal had to live there. It was where their jobs, homes, and families were. Without a great deal of help, it would have been nearly impossible for most residents to move. And as Lois Gibbs pointed out, how can you sell a house that no person of sound mind would buy? How do you make a mortgage payment and a rent payment when you bring home only so much money? These are just a couple of the serious questions that hundreds of residents had to face on a daily basis. They felt that not only their health was in danger but also their livelihood.

Mothers like Lois Gibbs watched their children suffer with unusual diseases. Fathers watched helplessly as their wives endured miscarriages. Families watched their homes slowly fall apart as the chemicals seeped in and around their homes, causing paint to peel and wood to rot. Everyone with children experienced the closing of schools and a feeling of hopelessness.

Some scientists were brought in by both the LCHA and the EPA. Often the tests showed there were some abnormalities. In certain areas, birth weights were low and miscarriages higher than normal. The chromosome test that the EPA gave also showed that about 36 families had broken chromosomes. A rare disorder, it meant these families had a greater chance of developing cancer, birth defects, miscarriages, and more. To make matters worse, those children affected could pass the chromosomal defect to future generations. These findings heightened the already growing fear that plagued Love Canal residents. They were certain their health was in jeopardy because of the chemicals. Nearly two years of testing, both on the residents and in their homes, media hype, and an outspoken mother named Lois Gibbs allowed the residents room and time to let their own fears develop. Did they have a legitimate cause to feel frightened? Were they overreacting? Some believe so.

On the other side of the story are the people who don't live at the Love Canal, the scientists and the government officials at the state and federal levels. Some scientists felt that many, if not all, the tests given were mishandled in some way. Even the tests performed by the scientist

Dr. Paigen, who worked closely with Lois Gibbs, did not yield results that made sense. For example, air samples showed the presence of only 8 chemicals, even though there were more than 200 chemicals in the canal.

Another study, in support of the swale theory, conducted by Lois Gibbs and Dr. Vianna, eventually showed that women who lived in low-lying areas and near wetlands experienced more miscarriages than normal, and their children had lower than normal birth weights. The study was wholly scientific. Lois made maps of the swale areas and marked on them the homes where these problems occurred. By looking at the maps, one could make an assumption that chemicals were getting into the water and contaminating families who lived near these areas. Lois also marked other illnesses on her map to show that there were more respiratory problems to the north of the Canal, which coincided with the direction of the area's prevailing winds. To the south of the Love Canal, there were swampy areas, and there, too, more than the expected number of miscarriages and birth defects occurred. Two questions that arise when looking at these studies are how accurate are the studies? And what is normal?

When a scientific study is undertaken, scientists and, in this case, doctors, don't analyze just one group, the group of people who are affected. Rather, the affected group, and at least one other or two groups, called "control groups," are studied. The control groups must be similar to the study group in such aspects as age and background. In the case of one study, members of the control group lived relatively close to the Love Canal, although a few miles up river.

There has been tremendous debate about how the studies were conducted and how reliable they really were. In an article written by Dr. Michael Kirsch, he cited the *Washington Post* as stating that, 20 years after the initial evacuation, the allegations that the chemicals at the disposal site have had long-term adverse health effects on former residents have not been adequately substantiated. The article said there was no evidence that exposure to the chemicals had caused any of the frequently cited health problems of which the Love Canal residents of the 1970s complained.

No evidence? What about all the studies that were done? What about the illnesses—strange and rare—that the residents experienced? Were they not real? Dr. Kirsch stated further that the studies were based largely on anecdotal information provided by questionnaires submitted to a narrowly selected group of residents; there were no adequate control groups, and the claims the illnesses had been caused by chemical pollution were not medically validated.

In 1980, a panel of scientists convened by New York's governor discussed the effects of chemicals on the Love Canal residents and whether or not the studies that had been done were even accurately stated. The panel stated, in reference to one of the studies, "It is based largely on anecdotal information provided by questionnaires submitted to a narrowly selected group of residents. It cannot be taken seriously as a piece of sound epidemiological research." In short, the studies and surveys conducted by Lois and those scientists she worked with were worthless. They had no sound backing, no legitimate scientific proof.

A closer look at some of the studies poses arguments from both sides. In May 1978 the New York State Department of Health was ordered to begin a study after receiving the results of EPA environmental monitoring. It was felt that a detailed health profile of

The New York State Department began conducting tests to determine the health profile of Love Canal residents. Testing began in 1978. Beginning three years after the testing, the media and the government became skeptical of the results. Senator Daniel Patrick Moynihan holds up a report that points out the problems with the original Love Canal studies.

all the residents who lived or had lived in the Love Canal area was needed. A 20-page questionnaire was given door-to-door to residents. Blood samples were also taken. The results showed women who lived at the Love Canal were more likely to experience miscarriages than those who did not. A state of emergency was declared at this time. But what control group was used to make these comparisons? The first two rings of families living in the area surrounding the Love Canal were relocated.

A second study was conducted in addition to this one because residents living outside the affected area were not happy with the results of the first. This study, led by Dr. Paigen, was done via telephone. The survey area was larger than in the previous study, and again people were asked about their health.

Many adverse health effects were found in greater frequency in wet areas than in dry areas. Wet areas were those bordered by streams or swales, both of which could form a transport system for harmful chemicals. Miscarriages, birth defects, asthma, urinary disease, and suicide were all far more likely in wet areas. This study, however, was criticized by many scientists for the many weaknesses in the way it was designed.

The same holds true with the test the EPA conducted regarding chromosomal defects. The U.S. Department of Justice initiated this study to gather evidence against Hooker Chemical, the company that originally dumped much of the toxic material into the canal. The Justice Department wanted Hooker to pay for the relocation of the Love Canal residents. The problem with this study was the EPA didn't have the funding for a control group and so based their investigation on historical information.

A follow-up study by Dr. Paigen in 1980 confirmed her theory about the wetland areas. Her study included a questionnaire that was distributed to not only the local residents of the Love Canal but also a control group similar in size located in the Niagara Falls area. Her results showed that problems were statistically higher in the Love Canal area.

Many people believe there was just cause to relocate the residents living immediately around the canal, the families in Rings 1 and 2. Many also feel the 1980 evacuation was unnecessary, and, according to an article written by Michael Fumento, *EPA Hides Behind Myths of Love Canal*, study after study conducted by the federal government and the New York State Department of Health found that the Love Canal residents had no more illnesses than would be expected in any other area of similar size.

A *New York Times* editorial in 1981 suggested the public would have suffered less from the chemicals than from the hysteria generated by flimsy research irresponsibly handled.

One study conducted by the Department of Health and Human Services related to an increased incidence of miscarriages. Dr. Arthur Bloom, a geneticist who helped evaluate a previous study, said, "Those studies were the most definitive, positive studies—the only ones that stood good scientific tests."

If one study, valid and true, showed there was a problem with miscarriages in relation to the amounts of toxic chemicals in the area, wouldn't this be enough evidence of a health problem? Although some would disagree, the answer is no. Especially when talking about relocating hundreds of families at a cost reaching high into the millions of dollars. There had to be more proof—solid, valid, scientific proof—and it just wasn't there.

Michael Brown, the reporter who originally wrote the stories about the Love Canal in the *Niagara Gazette,* wrote an article in July 1989 for the *Atlantic Monthly* entitled *A Toxic Ghost Town*. He recounts the events that took place at the Love Canal between 1978 and 1980 and seems to recognize the shortcomings of many of the studies conducted earlier. He, too, refers to the studies mentioned above and notes that, generally speaking, respiratory disease was higher in the entire region because of the high degree of industrial pollution in this part of New York State. He quotes Congressman LaFalce as admitting that decisions were made regarding the second evacuation in 1980 on "soft or no data at all."

Lois Gibbs, the once quiet housewife, remained under attack for her actions at the Love Canal. She was accused of exaggerating health problems and seeking celebrity status by appearing on television and the radio programs. Some feel she used propaganda and illegal measures to get her way. (*Propaganda,* according to *Merriam-Webster's Dictionary,* is defined as "ideas, facts, or allegations spread deliberately to further one's cause or to damage an opposing cause.") After all, she did hold two EPA officials hostage, and she let residents know about the studies and health effects even though they were not considered reliable. But did her tactics work? Lois Gibbs and many residents thought so. They saw the fight as frustrating and time consuming. Meanwhile, people were getting sick and children were suffering. Lois Gibbs was a housewife who would stop at nothing to spare her children and others any more hardship. She saw the evidence every day when residents came to her house and office, complaining of pain and worried about their future. In the end, they were relocated.

The Superfund Program was created in 1980 by Congress to help locate and clean up dump sites across the United States. The Program was a direct result of the problem at the Love Canal, and the growing awareness among Americans that the toxic waste being dumped on and beneath the land was a serious health threat. The EPA oversees the operations of Superfund, but in years past it was accused of mismanagement and corruption. The other big question was whether the EPA really helped or hurt the residents of the Love Canal.

It is always easier to look at a problem and its resolution with hindsight. It is easier to see where one might have done things differently. Confusion ran rampant throughout the homes and lives of the Love

Workers demolish houses in the Love Canal neighborhood. Families eventually relocated with aid from the government.

Canal residents. Fear directed them in their cause.

Who is to blame for the problems at the Love Canal? Should a multimillion dollar company be responsible just because they make a lot of money? Should the City of Niagara Falls and the school board be held responsible because they built a community on land they knew was contaminated?

Hooker Chemical was deeply involved with lawsuits against them and has had to change its name to Occidental Chemical because of all the bad publicity. Occidental has stood its ground in stating that no adverse health effects can be proved to be a consequence of waste disposed in the Love Canal. It also maintains that it was not the company's fault, because it fully disclosed information about the buried chemicals when it sold the land to the city and school board. The chemical company kept no secrets from the city, but the city kept secrets from the people who bought homes on top of the canal. In 1995 CNN reported that the U.S. government announced a settlement with Occidental Chemical Corporation for the cleanup costs associated with the Love Canal. Occidental was directed to pay $129 million to settle the case; $28 million was interest and the remainder was for reimbursement to the government for cleaning up the site and relocating about 1,000 families.

At the time Hooker Chemical was disposing of the chemicals, it was doing so in accordance with existing laws. Between 1942 and 1954, little was known about toxic and hazardous chemicals, and burying them in metal barrels was thought to be the safest way to get rid of them. Moreover, Hooker sold the land, making it clearly known that homes should not be built on the land. The City of Niagara Falls did so anyway.

Part of this debate relates also to industry versus environment. We all enjoy the convenience that plastic and other chemically based items provide to our everyday lives. But we must not forget that with this convenience comes the toxic and hazardous chemical by-products that result from the manufacture of these items. Unfortunately, technology and science have not yet come up with entirely safe methods for disposal of these toxic chemical by-products.

Michael Brown said in his article, "One of the biggest arguments against Love Canal residents is this. People move in and out of cities and towns and families may suffer multiple ailments. The cause of many chemicals when they interact with one another is unknown and because survey populations are limited, attempts to prove a statistically significant effect is doomed for failure."

We have a long way to go in knowing the whole story about how the chemicals we are exposed to affect our entire bodily systems. Science has to play catch-up, and technology must be used to find other, safe ways to dispose of our toxic and hazardous wastes.

The debate about Love Canal will no doubt continue. If there is a bright side to the Love Canal tragedy, however, it is that we, as a nation, learned how serious the issue of hazardous waste disposal is to our future and the future of our children. The lessons learned at Love Canal have given us all new-found reasons to strive to make our planet a safer place to live.

Now What?

The foundation of the Heisner house is all that's left of in the once vibrant Love Canal community. The Heisner family moved to another part of the city and the house was demolished.

Politics versus science. This is how many of the residents at the Love Canal felt. It was a political issue more than anything else, and only when the residents of the Love Canal involved the media by putting pressure on political candidates and getting the word out did people like the governor of New York and the president of the United States act. To be fair, these politicians were concerned with the problems at the Love Canal, but they were also worried about how they might look to the nation. With an election coming up, the last thing Jimmy Carter needed was bad publicity and a reputation of not caring about the residents of the Love Canal. The LCHA protested at political conventions and gave hundreds of interviews to the media. They constantly asked candidates their position on hazardous waste issues and on Love Canal in particular. A grassroots campaign had been launched, and ultimately it led to a visit by Jimmy Carter to Love Canal.

Lois Gibbs said Jimmy Carter didn't want to spend millions of dollars on the Love Canal cleanup and relocation efforts but was forced to in order to gain votes from people concerned about hazardous waste and the outcome of the Love Canal. Gibbs felt that all decisions were based on political reasons, not scientific ones. And although she felt there was plenty of evidence, the previous chapter, "The Great Debate," shows there wasn't conclusive evidence, even in the minds of some scientists.

In 1980 the Superfund Program was developed in response to the devastation at the Love Canal. It was clear something had to be done, and an agency needed to be developed to monitor hazardous waste sites and clean them up. Congress established the Superfund Program as citizens grew more concerned about places like the Love Canal. The goal of Superfund is to locate, investigate, and clean up the worst sites nationwide. The EPA administers the Superfund Program along with individual states and local governments. The Superfund Program is still active today, and you can visit the Progams on the World Wide Web.

How does Superfund locate a site? First, a site discovery or notification to the EPA of the existence of possibly hazardous substances is made. People like you may be involved in discovering a hazardous waste site, or it may be discovered by a state agency or EPA regional office. Once discovered, sites are entered into the Comprehensive Environmental Response, Compensation, and Liability Information System (CERCLIS), the EPA's computerized inventory of potential hazardous substance release sites. The EPA then evaluates the potential for a release of hazardous substances from the site through several steps in the Superfund cleanup process: These steps are as follows:

- **Preliminary Assessment/Site Inspection (PA/SI)**—investigations of site conditions
- **HRS Scoring**—screening mechanism used to place sites on the National Priorities List (NPL)
- **NPL Site Listing Process**—list of the most serious sites identified for possible long-term cleanup
- **Remedial Investigation/Feasibility Study (RI/FS)**—determines the nature and extent of contamination
- **Record of Decision (ROD)**—explains which cleanup alternatives will be used at NPL sites
- **Remedial Design/Remedial Action (RD/RA)**—preparation and implementation of plans and specifications for applying site remedies
- **Construction Completion**—identifies completion of cleanup activities
- **Operation and Maintenance (O&M)**—conducted after site actions are complete to ensure that all actions are effective and operating properly
- **NPL Site Deletions**—removal of sites from the NPL

Preliminary Assessment investigates readily available information about a site and its surrounding area. This assessment is designed to distinguish what sites pose a threat to humans and the environment and what sites do not pose a threat. If the PA results recommend further investigation, a site inspection is performed.

Site Inspection identifies sites that qualify for further investigation. Investigators collect environmental and waste hazards to determine what kinds of hazardous waste are found at a particular site.

> *HRS Scoring* stands for the Hazard Ranking System. It is a mathematical model that determines the risk to the public and the environment. Points are awarded to a site based on the chemicals it contains, how close it is to communities, water sources, and wildlife.

The EPA uses information from the Preliminary Assessment and Site Inspection to assess the potential threat to human health or the environment. Several factors are used in determining the score, such as:

- the likelihood that a site has released or has the potential to release hazardous substances into the environment;

- characteristics of the waste (e.g., toxicity and waste quantity); and people or sensitive environments (targets) affected by the release.

The ways in which chemicals may enter the human body and environment are also scored. They include: groundwater migration (drinking water), surface-water migration, (drinking water, human food chain, sensitive environments), soil exposure (resident and nearby populations, sensitive environments), and air migration (population, sensitive environments). As we saw at the Love Canal, the ways in which hazardous chemicals entered the environment and body included all four of these factors.

If all pathway scores are low, the site score is low. However, the site score can be relatively high even if only one pathway score is high. This is an important factor in HRS scoring, because some extremely dangerous sites pose threats through only one pathway.

Workers dig up contaminated dirt in the back yard of Love Canal residents. Chemicals can enter the human body in a variety of ways, sometimes through foods that were exposed to toxic chemicals. Many residents of the Love Canal ate fruits and vegetables they grew in their backyards. These foods may have contained dioxin.

NPL Site Listing Process, or the National Priorities List, is occurs once the above steps are taken. It simply determines which sites warrant further investigation and notifies the public of those sites the EPA feels need further investigation. The NPL is available to the public on the Superfund website at *http://www.epa.gov/superfund/sites/npl/npl.htm.* By simply clicking on a state on the map of the United States, areas listed by county, then by town or street may be viewed. The NPL Site Listing for the Love Canal may be viewed at: *http://www.epa.gov/region02/superfnd/site_sum/0201290c.htm.*

Remedial Investigation/Feasibility Study collects data to characterize site conditions, determine the nature of the waste, assess risk to human health and the environment, and conduct treatability testing to evaluate the cost of the treatment technologies being considered.

Record of Decision is a public document that explains which cleanup alternatives will be used to clean up a Superfund site.

Remedial Design and Remedial Action is the step where technical specifications and technologies are designed. Remedial Action follows RD and involves the actual construction phase of the site cleanup.

Construction Completion is a list that categorizes sites and their successful completion of cleanup activities. At this point the actual cleanup is almost finished and the site is being qualified for deletion from the NPL.

Operation and Maintenance is the step at which the state or potentially responsible party maintains the site by inspecting it, sampling and analyzing the site, and reporting its findings.

NPL Site Deletions occur when the EPA determines that a site is no longer a threat to human health or the environment. All appropriate action has been taken and the Superfund has done all it can to insure the safety of human health and the environment.

You can see why it would take years to complete all these steps. This is one of the good things that has come out of the Love Canal disaster. Generally, citizens of the

The streets of the City of Niagara Falls have remained silent for many years. Most of the 900 families living in the area relocated because of the Love Canal situation.

United States are more aware of hazardous waste and sites around the country and are willing to take a stand against the government and corporations.

The Love Canal residents have long since been relocated. All but 67 of the 900 families have moved from the Love Canal to start their lives over. Lois Gibbs is among those who left. She moved to Virginia. In her book she points out that many marriages were stressed by the crisis and didn't survive, including her own. Lois and her husband Harry divorced because Harry wanted his old life back, a wife who wanted to be a housewife, a regular schedule, and a simple lifestyle. Lois felt she should continue with her efforts, helping people of other communities. Sick children, meetings, worry and fear, changing schools, doctors' visits, a feeling of losing control, and a change in the normal routine of family life were all factors that affected the lives of the residents. Teenagers suffered with the change of schools, forcing them to leave not only a familiar place but also their good friends.

Some people thought by moving from the Love Canal their illnesses would get better or go away. For some they did, but others remained ill. There is still the looming question, What will happen in the future? No one, not even scientists or doctors, know what the diseases will do or if former residents will develop a disease later in life. Lois Gibbs said in her book that, when she takes her kids to the doctor, she holds her breath until they get a clean bill of health. Lois says it's like sitting on a time bomb—you never know when something will hit, when a disease will show itself and take over.

Many of the residents of the Love Canal feel they don't belong in their new homes and neighborhoods. It's been hard for them to reestablish their roots and become a part of the area. Barbara Quimby, who was born and raised in the Love Canal, said, "Love Canal will always be home for me." She feels like an outsider in her new world.

In an effort to help others, Lois Gibbs founded the Center for Health, Environment, and Justice, which provides direct assistance to families and communities facing environmental problems. She warns that what happened to the people of the Love Canal could happen to you. After all, just take a look at the EPA's National Priorities List and you will be surprised by the number of sites in each state. Through the Center for Health,

Environment, and Justice, Lois has visited many states and seen cases much worse than that of the Love Canal. Lakes have been destroyed, drinking supplies ruined, children suffer from cancer, asthma, and learning disabilities, and much more. If anything good is to come out of the Love Canal, it is that our awareness and handling of toxic and hazardous wastes has been much improved. However, we still have a long way to go. The Love Canal problem is still not over.

In 1988 sections of the Love Canal neighborhood were declared "habitable." Gibbs reminds us there is a difference between habitable and safe. She feels this declaration is illegal and moving people back to the area despicable. Procedures used to determine the habitability of the Love Canal were greatly flawed. The studies were manipulated to show the public that a toxic and hazardous waste site could be cleaned up and reused. Gibbs feels once an area is contaminated, there is no way to remove all the chemicals.

Two hundred homes that remain on the north side of the Love Canal are being sold to families. Gibbs believes these homes are still contaminated. Some cleanup efforts have occurred, but these homes are next to contaminated and uninhabitable homes. All that separates them is a street.

Gibbs refers to an amendment made in 1986 called SARA, or the Superfund Amendment and Reauthorization Act. This act was used to increase funding into the Superfund, and it was increased to $8.5 billion. Section 312 of SARA specifically requires the EPA to assess the risks associated with inhabiting the Love Canal Emergency Declaration Area. The Habitability Report fails to do this and as a result, Gibbs believes moving people back is illegal. Gibbs feels that at least a reproductive risk assessment should have been done. In all the health studies that were done at the Love Canal, damage to the fetus and risks to young children were clearly documented. These studies were also the basis of two evacuations ordered by the state health commissioner. Because there has been no reproductive risk assessment, there is no way to judge whether these risks have changed since the evacuations were ordered. Allowing families to move back in could result in health problems, especially in pregnant women and young children.

Today there are many laws protecting us from pollution and toxic and chemical waste. Some laws, such as the Federal Water Pollution Control Act, were established in the late 1940s but amended in more recent years. The new laws and amendments to old ones have come about as we have become more aware of the hazards of toxic chemicals.

Other laws include the Safe Drinking Water Act (1974), Toxic Substances Control Act (1976), and the Community Right to Know Act (1986). The Community Right to Know Act is important because it allows citizens to access information about hazardous chemicals in their communities. The act requires companies to identify chemicals stored in a community and explain the health effects of these chemicals. Although it is important for the public to know what is going on in their communities, recently this law has come under heavy debate. The act requires an estimated 66,000 U.S. chemical facilities to produce a record of their inventories, accident histories, and worst-case scenarios. With this act, the EPA planned on making this information public, displaying it on the World Wide Web. The chemical facilities did not like this idea and claimed that the risk of Internet terrorism would be far worse than a chemical disaster. Imagine a terrorist sitting in another country and gaining control of a facility via a computer or infecting the facilities computers with a virus. Another worst-case scenario and a real concern is terrorists actually attacking these facilities. Because of the World Trade Center and Pentagon attacks by terrorists, many people don't want this information made public, especially on the Web, where it may be easily retrieved. If a terrorist knows where a chemical plant is located and what kind of chemicals it produces, the chemical plant could become a target. It is easy to imagine the danger our lives would be in if a chemical plant producing toxic and hazardous chemicals was suddenly blown up or caught on fire. This is yet another new and ongoing debate that we must face in light of terrorist activities in the United States.

How Can We Make a Difference?

So often the problem seems too big for us to be able to handle individually. Making a difference in the fight against toxic and chemical hazards seems like too much of a job for one person, or for even a few. However, with the combined efforts of companies, the chemical industries, and individuals, we can all make a difference. It starts with awareness. The awareness brought about in part by the Love Canal incident has taught the citizens of the United States and other countries the importance of disposing of chemicals and waste properly. It has allowed companies to rethink the way in which they manufacture a product and dispose of the by-products and waste. Some plastic manufacturers and consumer product companies are setting up plastic recycling programs. Today we know the importance of recycling our plastic bottles, aluminum cans, and paper goods. Consumers can help reduce waste just by recycling at home. The recycling programs set up by local governments reflect a keen awareness of the ongoing problems regarding waste.

The Love Canal disaster raised issues of toxic waste disposal. Today companies have improved the containers for storing chemicals and changed the way they dispose of chemicals.

The pollution that affected the Love Canal and so many other areas across the United States as industries commonly dumped their waste into waterways is being controlled. Pollution control laws now limit the materials that industries can dump into surface water. The laws have made a huge difference and greatly reduced water pollution, but some feel they aren't enough. The good news is things are changing for the better. The bad news is, we have a long way to go.

Modern technology also has a lot of catching up to do. Currently we do have some pollution-fighting technology like Goop Gobblers. Scientists have discovered strains of bacteria that feed on oil and other toxic pollutants. Bacteria have been used to clean up oil spills and agricultural runoff. The problem is that sometimes the bacteria work too slowly or not at all. Introducing bacteria into areas where they aren't naturally found may disrupt the ecosystems.

Instead of using pesticides, some fruit farmers use the Bug Vac. It is a giant vacuum tool used to suck bugs and insects off fruit without causing damage. The downside is that it removes all bugs, even the good ones that benefit the plants and soil.

Smoke Scrubbers are used in coal-burning power plants. Lime and water are sprayed into smokestacks, rinsing out the sulfur dioxide, which causes acid rain. The problem is it produces a toxic sludge that must be disposed of.

Residents of towns and cities can also make a difference. In some cities across the country, an "amnesty day" is declared. The word *amnesty* means to grant forgiveness. For example, in Seminole County, Florida, authorities offer a free disposal day. Residents are encouraged to dispose of their household hazardous waste such as paint, household cleaners, and tires. This is a great way to encourage people to take care of their hazardous waste properly and also to educate them about hazardous waste.

With each solution, however, comes a new problem and challenge. Today, children are breathing more toxic and hazardous chemicals than ever before in history. Sites like the Love Canal are found not only in our country but also all over the world. The threat of chemical waste bombards us on a daily basis. It is a problem that will only get worse in time without continued intervention, not just from the government and industries but also from people like you.

The Love Canal disaster happened over 20 years ago, but its effect on our lives remains strong today. Many people suffered not just physically but also mentally. We can only hope lessons were learned from such incidents and progress continues to be made in the fight against hazardous materials and toxic chemicals. The fact remains that our society isn't going to change how it produces and manufactures goods. We've become a throw-away society, wanting the convenience of buying things and throwing them away without reusing or recycling them. Plastic has become a mainstay in our everyday lives, but not without a cost. We can change how we live individually. We can become aware of the world around us and take action at home by watching what we use and how we dispose of it.

The debate over the Love Canal will continue, as will that of many other sites. The Love Canal opened America's eyes to the problem of toxic and hazardous waste. Although the Love Canal disaster devastated many people's lives, it also made us more aware of the problem and gave us a determination to take action and make our world safe.

Chronology

1757	The region's early explorers and settlers note the river's potential for inexpensive waterpower. A tiny canal is built for a sawmill.
1879	Using hydroelectric power, Niagara Falls is lit up at night for tourists.
1890s	William T. Love has an idea for an industrial city. A canal will be the center of the city, on the shores of Lake Ontario. A factory is built, as are a few homes, and the ground is broken for the canal.
Mid-1890s	Investigators withdraw dollars from the Love project because of a depression in the economy. Congress passes an environmental bill rejecting removal of water from the Niagara River, in order to preserve the waterfall. The canal is left as a 60 foot wide, 10 foot deep, 3,000 foot long monument, fed by rivulets and creeks of the Niagara River. The drainage trench leading into the river is used for play, swimming, and fishing.
1920	The Hooker Chemical Corporation buys the canal site at public auction.
1942	The Niagara Power and Development Company, successor to the Niagara County Irrigation and Water Supply Development Company, gives Hooker permission to dispose of wastes in the canal, and Hooker begins disposal.
1945	Hooker racks up $19 million in sales.
1947	Hooker buys the 16-acre dump site.
1952	The City of Niagara Falls disposes of municipal wastes at the site.
1953	The Love Canal is nearly full. The site is covered with earth/clay, and weeds grow over it.
April 28, 1953	The Niagara Falls school board purchases the 16 acres, including the canal, for $1.00.
January 1954	Construction work begins over the old canal, including streets and the 99th Street Elementary School.

Chronology

1955	The 99th Street Elementary School is completed and has 400 children attending every day. The school board sells 6.58 acres of the northern end of the property to the City of Niagara Falls.
1958	Three or four children suffer chemical burns at the old Love Canal property.
1960s	Construction on blue-collar residential neighborhoods and low-income apartments explodes around the canal and residents arrive in the area.
1962	The school board sells 5.98 acres at the southern end of the canal to a New York City resident, who further complicates the situation by selling it to someone in Pennsylvania.
1965	Residents begin expressing concern to city officials about the black, oily substance in their basement sump pumps, but nothing is done.
1969	City records indicate a number of complaints. Records also show that city building inspectors examined an area at or near the Love Canal dump site.
1970s	The last group of new homes is sold. They sell from $18,000 to $23,000. Residents are not warned of any dangers to their health.
1976	The International Joint Commission, representing the Canadian and U.S. governments, monitors the conditions of the Great Lakes. The commission detects traces of the insecticide Mirix in Lake Ontario fish, and, soon after, the New York State health commissioner issues a warning that Lake Ontario fish are unsafe for consumption. The New York State Department of Environmental Conservation finds one source of Mirix traced to Niagara Falls and the 102nd Street dump site, next to the Love Canal.
October 1976	The *Niagara Gazette* places coverage of the history of the Love Canal landfill on the front page.

Chronology

Late fall 1976, early winter 1977	In response to various news articles, the Department of Environmental Conservation continues investigations on chemicals in the area.
April 1977	A Calspan survey shows that 21 of 188 homes adjacent to the canal have varying degrees of chemical residue in their sump pumps. There are strong odors, and 75 percent of the affected homes are at the southern section of the Love Canal site. It is also stated that storm sewers to the west of the canal contain PCBs. It is revealed that there are areas of the Love Canal where drums of chemicals buried at depths of three feet or less have corroded, and many are exposed at the surface. It is also noted that chemicals are leaking from the drums and are sometimes visible at the surface.
Summer 1977	News coverage of the Love Canal situation increases.
September 1977	U.S. Congressman John LaFalce tours the area and is discouraged by what he sees and hears. He comes again in late September with members of the EPA.
October 1977	An EPA consultant samples the air in the basements of the Love Canal homes.
1978	Hooker, whose Niagara location is both its largest and its headquarters, becomes a division of Occidental Petroleum Corporation.
Spring, Summer 1978	Residents are becoming aware of the problem at the Love Canal and start to attend meetings. Lois Gibbs forms the Love Canal Homeowners Association (LCHA). President Carter declares a state of emergency in the area and approves emergency financial aid.
Spring 1978	The EPA continues to sample air in home basements. Personnel from the regional Department of Environmental Conservation sample basement sump pumps and the storm sewers next to the Love Canal. The storm sewers' waters run untreated into the river. Soil samples showing alarming levels of hazardous chemicals are discovered by Dr. David Axelrod, the state health department's director of laboratory sciences. He informs Robert Whalen, the health commissioner, that the area is in extreme danger of serious health threats.

Chronology

April 13, 1978	Dr. Whalen declares a relocation of women and children living in Ring 1 (people whose backyards border the canal area on 97th and 99th Streets and face the strip of Colvin Boulevard between the two streets) and Ring 2 (homes across the street from Ring 1 homes on 97th and 99th Streets). He also declares the closing of the 99th Street School.
Second week of May 1978	The EPA says that the toxic vapors in people's basements pose serious health hazards.
June 1978	Blood samples are taken from residents whose backyards are next to the canal.
June, July 1978	A flimsy fence is placed around part of the canal area to imply it is dangerous. No Trespassing signs are also put up.
August 1978	Residents are told to stop eating vegetables and fruits from their gardens because the produce is harmful. They are told to keep their children from going barefoot and going into their basements. The government continues to force residents to live in the area while doing its tests related to possible health effects. The New York State Department of Health advises pregnant women to leave the area.
August 7, 1978	The president of the United States declares the Love Canal neighborhood an emergency area and provides funds to permanently relocate the 239 families living in the first two rings of homes that encircle the landfill site. Families in the remaining 10-block area, including Lois Gibbs and her family, are told they are not at risk.
February 8, 1979	The New York State Department of Health expands the study population and reports increased frequencies of adverse reproductive effects in women and recommends all pregnant women and children less than two years of age evacuate.
September 8, 1979	Three hundred additional families living within the 10-block neighborhood are temporarily relocated as a result of health problems caused by chemical exposures from the cleanup activities.

April 1980	Robert Abrams, attorney general for New York State, files a $635 million lawsuit against Occidental Petroleum Corporation and Hooker Chemical Corporation, with the defendants being charged with negligence in preventing the migration of wastes and in failing to warn the public of the Love Canal hazards.
May 17,1980	The EPA announces the result of blood tests, which show chromosomal damage in the Love Canal residents. Residents are told that this means they have an increased risk of cancer, reproductive problems, and genetic damage.
May 19, 1980	The Love Canal residents are frightened by the news of chromosomal damage and angered by the lack of government action to relocate their families from the serious public health risks of living near the Love Canal; they hold two EPA representatives hostage. The Love Canal families demand that the White House relocate all families by noon Wednesday, May 21, 1980.
May 21, 1980	The White House agrees to evacuate all the Love Canal families temporarily until permanent relocation funds can be secured. President Carter declares a second federal emergency in the Love Canal area. The Love Canal Revitalization Agency is created. The Comprehensive Environmental Response, Compensation, and Liability Act (Superfund) is enacted.
October 1, 1980	President Carter visits the City of Niagara Falls to sign the appropriation bill that provides the funding for permanent relocation of all 900 families who wish to leave.
December 20, 1983	A lawsuit filed by 1,328 the Love Canal residents is settled for just under $20 million with Occidental Chemical Corporation, a subsidiary of Occidental Petroleum. One million dollars is set aside for a medical trust fund.
September 1988	The New York State Department of Health completes a five-year habitability study and concludes that portions of the Love Canal neighborhood are "as habitable as other areas of the City of Niagara Falls." The department refuses to declare these areas unsafe.

Chronology

September 15, 1989	People from across the country join former Love Canal residents at the capitol in Albany, New York, to protest the decision to move new families into the Love Canal area.
January 19, 1990	Lois Gibbs and others meet with the EPA administrator, William Reilly, in an attempt to block the resettlement of the northern portion of the Love Canal.
April 1, 1990	Community leaders from across the state and nation come together with one-time residents of the Love Canal in a major rally in the City of Niagara Falls to protest the resettlement.
August 15, 1990	The Love Canal Revitalization Agency renames a portion of the Love Canal Black Creek Village and announces that nine homes are available for sale to the general public.
November 28, 1990	The first new family moves into the Love Canal, but further efforts to sell homes make slow gains. Regional banks are unwilling to accept mortgages for Love Canal homes.
April 1992	The Federal Housing Administration agrees to provide mortgage insurance to families who wish to purchase Love Canal homes.
June 22, 1994	Occidental Petroleum agrees to pay $129 million to cover the federal government's cleanup costs at the Love Canal.
January 5, 1995	Occidental Chemical, a subsidiary of Occidental Petroleum, takes over full operations and maintenance of the chemical waste treatment plant at the Love Canal.

Further Reading

Colten, Craig E, Skinner, Peter. *The Road to Love Canal: Managing Industrial Waste Before EPA.* Texas: University of Texas Press, 1996.

Gano, Lila. *Hazardous Waste.* San Diego, CA: Lucent Books, 1991.

Gibbs, Lois Marie. *Love Canal: The Story Continues.* Canada: New Society Publishers, 1998.

National Wildlife Federation. *Pollution, Problems and Solutions.* Philadelphia: Chelsea House, 1997

Sherrow, Victoria. *Love Canal: Toxic Waste Tragedy.* New Jersey; Enslow Publishers. July 2001.

Organizations to contact:

Citizen's Clearinghouse for Hazardous Waste
PO Box 926
Arlington, VA 22216

Environmental Protection Agency
Public Information Center
401 M St. SW
Washington, DC 20460
www.epa.org

Envirolink
5808 Forbes Ave. 2nd Floor
Pittsburgh, PA 15217
www.envirolink.org

Friends of the Earth
1025 Vermont Ave. NW
Washington, DC 20005
www.foe.org

Greenpeace USA
1436 U St. NW
Washington, DC 20009

The Sierra Club
730 Polk St.
San Francisco, CA 94109

Bibliography

Websites:

http://dencities.com/eriecanal.html - Erie Canal history

http://www4.cnn.com/US/9808/07/love.canal/index.html - CNN Residents Return

http://www.epa.gov/superfund/about.htm - About Superfund

http://www.infoniagara.com/f-river.html - Niagara River info

http://www.iaw.com/~falls/power.html - Niagara Falls and river history

http://ublib.buffalo.edu/libraries/units/sel/exhibits/lovecanal.html#About - has a nice map showing canal in relation to surrounding area.

http://ublib.buffalo.edu/libraries/units/archives/pbrown/ - photos

http://ublib.buffalo.edu/libraries/units/archives/pbrown/links.html - archives

http://www.niagara-info.com/historic.htm

http://www.iaw.com/~falls/origins.html#Power

http://www.encyclopedia.com/articles/22221.html - definition of horse power

http://mimas.csuchico.edu/~tm5/map.htm - Has a map that might be used in book

http://mimas.csuchico.edu/~tm5/physical.htm - information about Hooker Chemical and some history

http://cems.alfred.edu/students98/allansm/Onemoretry.html - what happened at Love Canal?

http://www.globalserve.net/~spinc/atomcc/dump.htm - the Love Canal Dump

http://www.cementkiln.com/downwinders/factsheet.html - Downwinders at risk

http://www.state.ny.us.edgesuite.net/governor/press/epa.html

http://www.epa.gov/oerrpage/superfund/sites/query/rods/r0288055.htm - Superfund

http://www.onlineethics.com/cases/l.canal/studies.html - pilot studies at Love Canal

http://www.townhall.com/edpage/columnists/fumento/fume122895.html - article

http://gladstone.uoregon.edu/~caer/lois_gibbs.html - Lois Gibbs

http://www.health.state.ny.us/nysdoh/environ/lovecan.htm - Love Canal study 1997

http://arts.envirolink.org/arts_and_activism/LoisGibbs.html

http://ublib.buffalo.edu/libraries/projects/lovecanal/ - Love Canal collection by Buffalo State University.

Bibliography

http://www.epa.gov/region02/superfnd/site_sum/0201290c.htm - Love Canal/EPA

http://www.globalserve.net/~spinc/atomcc/today.htm - Love Canal today

http://www.cato.org/pubs/regulation/reg19n2h.html - Dioxin Drama

http://history.acusd.edu/gen/nature/lovecanal.html - Love Canal

http://www.spa3.k12.sc.us/WebQuests/LoveCanal/ - Love Canal debate

http://www.ejnet.org/dioxin/ - Dioxin Homepage

Books:

Baines, John. *Environmental Disasters*. New York: Thomas Learning 1993.

Colten, Craig E, Skinner, Peter. *The Road to Love Canal: Managing Industrial Waste Before EPA.* Texas: University of Texas Press, 1996.

Gano, Lila. *Hazardous Waste.* San Diego, CA: Lucent Books, 1991.

Gibbs, Lois Marie. *Love Canal: The Story Continues.* Canada: New Society Publishers, 1998.

National Wildlife Federation. *Pollution, Problems and Solutions*. Philadelphia: Chelsea House, 1997

Love Canal. *A special report to the Governor and Legislature.* April 1981. State of New York.

Setterberg, Fred. *Toxic Nation*. New York: John Wiley and Sons, Inc, 1993

Skinner, Lawrence C. *Dioxins and Furans in Fish Below the Love Canal*. New York. New York State Department of Environmental Conservation. August 1993

Sherrow, Victoria. *Love Canal: Toxic Waste Tragedy*. New Jersey; Enslow Publishers. July 2001.

Streissguth, Thomas, editor. *Nuclear and Toxic Waste*. San Diego, CA : Greenhaven Press, 2001.

Index

Index

Index

Picture Credits

page

2: Associated Press, AP
10: © Bettmann/Corbis
12: Associated Press, AP
19: © Bettmann/Corbis
22: Associated Press, AP
26: Associated Press, AP
30: Courtesy of the Library of Congress
37: © Tim Wright/Corbis
40: Courtesy of the Environmental Protection Agency
44: Courtesy of the Central Intelligence Agency
47: University Archives, State University of New York at Buffalo
48: Associated Press, AP
50: Courtesy of the Environmental Protection Agency
53: Courtesy of the Environmental Protection Agency
62: Associated Press, AP
64: Courtesy of the Environmental Protection Agency
69: © Bettmann/Corbis
71: © Bettmann/Corbis
72: Associated Press, AP
74: Associated Press, The Daily Inter Lake
79: © Bettmann/Corbis
83: Courtesy of the Environmental Protection Agency
86: Associated Press, AP
91: University Archives, State University of New York at Buffalo
93: © Bettmann/Corbis
98: Associated Press, AP

Cover Photos: Associated Press, AP

JENNIFER BOND REED, author of over 100 stories and articles for children and parents, also publishes an online children's magazine with her husband, Jeff, called *Wee Ones E-magazine* (*www.weeonesmag.com*). She is an instructor for the Institute of Children's Literature and is currently writing two historical novels for children. Much of her time is spent writing and editing; however, her two children, Eric and Emma, keep her extremely busy. She lives in Maryland, enjoys traveling, and finding new things to write about.

JILL MCCAFFREY has served for four years as national chairman of the Armed Forces Emergency Services of the American Red Cross. Ms. McCaffrey also serves on the board of directors for Knollwood—the Army Distaff Hall. The former Jill Ann Faulkner, a Massachusetts native, is the wife of Barry R. McCaffrey, who served in President Bill Clinton's cabinet as director of the White House Office of National Drug Control Policy. The McCaffreys are the parents of three grown children: Sean, a major in the U.S. Army; Tara, an intensive care nurse and captain in the National Guard; and Amy, a seventh grade teacher. The McCaffreys also have two grandchildren, Michael and Jack.